100 Ideas for Art

Felicity Austin

Printing

Collage work

Painting

Drawing

Model-making and papier-mâché

Clay work

Weaving

Collins Educational
An Imprint of HarperCollins*Publishers*

Published 1998 by Collins Educational
77–85 Fulham Palace Road
London
W6 8JB

An imprint of HarperCollins*Publishers*

ISBN 000 3120147

Editor: Sue MacIntyre
Illustrations: Juliet Breese and Jean de Lemos
Cover photograph: Martin Soukias
Cover design: Clive Wilson
Text page design: The Design Works, Reading
Printed and bound: Martins the Printers Ltd, Berwick-on-Tweed

The author and publisher would like to thank Ajay, Anna, David, Duncan,
Edward, Emily, Esme, Fiona, Helen, Hester, Jamie, Jenny, John, Laura,
Lucy, Patrick, Peter, Ruth, Sam, Sarah, Sumeet, Tom and the children of
Stonygate School, Leicester for lending their artwork as a basis for the
illustrations in this book.
They would also like to thank the staff and children of Melcombe Primary
School, London, where the cover photograph was taken.

Contents

Introduction

Taught well, art is a wonderfully thought-provoking and problem-solving activity, engaging both the conscious thinking and more intuitive parts of the brain. The aim of this book is to offer worthwhile ideas for all kinds of artwork in the primary classroom, combining learning the necessary skills with an opportunity for self-expression. Both these aspects are vital. The ideas cover all the main areas of art you might expect to work on in the average primary classroom, and all have been tried and tested with children. Many offer a structured approach but within this there is great scope for children to express their own individuality. Many are individual activities, but there are group and class activities too, and some individual activities can easily be adapted for groups.

More details about working in the main areas of primary art: printing, collage work, painting, drawing, model-making and papier-mâché work, clay work and weaving will be found in the section introductions. These should be especially helpful to the non-specialist teacher.

A fruitful way of working (a format evolved over several years)

1 Demonstrate the new skill to be learnt to the whole class or group, and/or talk about the activity, the materials to be used, etc., to stimulate ideas.

2 Ask for the children's questions and comments.

3 Demonstrate any further techniques as necessary, accepting the children's suggestions and incorporating these into the demonstration if appropriate.

4 Put away your demonstration work so the children are not tempted to copy it.

5 Let the children start working and move among them, discussing what they're trying to achieve, making suggestions, etc, always acknowledging that the final decision is theirs as it's their work.

6 Have a short break halfway through the session. Encourage children to stand back from their work and evaluate its progress so far. Ask them to look at others' work, too, and to notice anything they think is interesting or works well. Point out some of these things to the class or group and hold up examples so that the children can learn from one another.

7 Let the children continue and finish off their work. (Older primary children often need encouragement to do this. As they become more aware, they often get to a stage where they achieve a partially successful work and are scared to finish it for fear of spoiling it.)

8 After clearing up, *look at the finished work with the children*. This is an invaluable part of the art lesson.

It reinforces what was learnt, boosts self-esteem, and teaches the children to assess their own and their classmates' work. Prepare some simple questions in advance to focus the children's looking. Bear in mind the criteria that were set for the activity and try to ascertain how successful the children have been at fulfilling them. With a whole class's work, the simplest way to look at it all is to get half the class to hold up their work while the other half look, and vice versa. (*See* idea 36 for a detailed example of this stage.)

If possible, stay with the children as they work. Art has been regarded as a subject that you could 'let the children get on with on their own'. But, if you arrange to be with the children as they work, you will be able to discuss problems as they arise, and possible solutions. For this reason I suggest that you often 'do art' with the whole class at a time.

Some projects are very messy but are well worth the mess for the experience and the enjoyment.

Using this book

Finding an idea

To help you find an appropriate idea, a summary of the scope, organisation needed, age range, time and any cross-curricular links for each idea is provided. Lists of equipment needed, over and above the normal classroom equipment of pencils, rulers, rubbers and scissors are also given. Some ideas do build on skills learnt in previous ones, and where this is so it is often indicated with a cross reference.

Time

The time given is the approximate working time needed for the activity, and does not include time for setting out materials and clearing up. It is offered as a rough guide only – there will always be children who work very quickly or very slowly.

Organisation

Again, details under this heading are suggestions only. Younger children, particularly in year 1, benefit greatly from working in a small group with adult support which gives scope for developing vocabulary, language and social skills. If you can't supervise the art group yourself, maybe you could train a volunteer parent for this role? Even with young children, some activities are suitable for doing with the whole class, if you have the facilities, and can arrange for an extra helper.

Photocopy masters

Where an idea has an accompanying photocopy master, there is a cross-reference to it in the teacher's notes.

Glossary

Armature
A framework that supports a sculpture or model. It can be made of any material: wire, card, wood, etc.

Bas-relief
A low carving on a flat surface in any material. For instance, the face of the queen on a coin is in bas-relief.

Biscuit-fire
See **Fire**.

Bubble print
A type of print taken from the bubbly surface of a bowl or tray of watery paint that has had washing up liquid added to it, then been blown through a straw, to create a pattern of bubbles on the surface of the liquid.

Collage
A picture or design made of pieces of various materials which have been stuck on to a background.

Collagraph
A print taken from a printing block on to which textured materials have been stuck. Although the process is usually done with a printing press and oil-based inks, experimental prints may be made at primary level in a simpler way.

Fire
To bake clay at a high temperature in a kiln to render the clay hard. Clay work is normally fired twice. The first firing is called a **biscuit-firing**, and work that has been fired once is hard but fairly brittle. A **glaze-firing** is a second firing at a higher kiln temperature than a biscuit-firing, during which the work that has been glazed is heated to a temperature which fuses or sets the glaze.

Glaze-fire
See **Fire**.

Impasto
The texture on the surface of a painting which has been created by the application of thick paint, using either a brush or a palette knife.

Impressed pattern, impression
A decorative pattern made in wet clay work with any tool which leaves an impression in the surface.

Marbling, marbled
A type of printing. At primary school level inks or diluted oil paint are floated on the surface of a tray of water. The water is stirred gently until a pattern forms in the inks. Paper is then laid on the surface of the water and this absorbs the ink or oil pattern.

Mono-print
Any method of printing from which it is only possible to take a single print.

Papier-mâché
A technique for making artifacts out of paper. Small pieces or strips of paper can be layered with paste, or a 'mash' of paper pulp can be made.

Rubbing
A way of transferring the pattern from a textured, incised or engraved surface on to a piece of paper. Paper is laid over the surface of the object from which a rubbing is to be taken, and a wax crayon, held on its side, is rubbed firmly over the paper. The pattern from the object underneath the paper emerges as a wax pattern on the paper.

Shade
Shades of a colour are the various 'versions' of that colour that can be mixed without adding white or black (*see also* **Tone** below). For instance, various shades of green from a yellowy green to a bluey green may be mixed from just one yellow and one blue.

Slip
A sloppy mixture of clay and water which helps to secure pieces of clay that are being joined together. Coloured slip can also be used to decorate clay work.

Stoneware clay
A type of clay which, when fired at temperatures above 1200°C, produces very hard non-porous pottery.

Stick-weaving
A weaving done using two or more sticks as a support to produce a decorative artifact.

Tone
Colours mixed with white give light tones of that colour, and colours mixed with black give dark tones of that colour. By adding more or less white a whole range of the light tones of, say, red may be mixed, from the palest pink to red itself, and the same with black to make dark tones.

Wax-resist
A process in which wax is used to prevent ink, dye or paint flooding on to all areas of paper or fabric. At primary level, this most often refers to the use of wax crayons used on paper which is then painted, but the term also encompasses the dyeing process known as batik, where patterns of melted wax are used to block out areas of cloth. The cloth is then immersed in dye. After dying the wax is removed, revealing the pattern.

Wedge
To thump a portion of clay hard to expel any air bubbles that there may be inside it. The clay is usually knocked against a table or work bench several times - a noisy but enjoyable process.

Printing

See pcm on page 76 for examples of printing techniques

Children need to learn that printing is making an impression in some way by pressing down and this is what distinguishes it from painting. Simple yet worthwhile printing techniques suitable for children of primary school age include:

● printing with natural objects (fruit and vegetable sections, etc.)

● junk printing, using all sorts of materials

● making and using simple stencils

● making simple printing blocks

● **mono-printing** of various kinds.

This section of the book includes activities using all these techniques. Through these varied experiences children will be exploring texture, line and composition, as well as learning about the different printing processes which will form the basis for more sophisticated types of printing at secondary level.

Encourage a thoughtful approach by providing rough paper to try out the printing tools provided and by encouraging the children to experiment with different effects, both before they start and while working on an activity. It is also important to offer the children the opportunity to build on earlier experiences while these are still fresh in their minds. You might do this, for example, by having a six week printing project for your art lessons so that the children can remember what was tried out in a previous lesson and build on it.

As discussed in the general Introduction, allow time to look at the work with the children at the end of each session, and to focus on what was asked of them and how this has been achieved.

The younger children are, the messier their early experiments will be and we should beware of imposing adult expectations on young children's work. Early printing experiments can be mounted, labelled and displayed just as they are, as 'Our experiments printing with bits and pieces of junk', or whatever is appropriate. All printing work in the first year of school will be experiments of some kind.

Even at this early stage, providing children with choices, either of tools, colour or subject matter, within the structure of the activity, is important. If the lesson is totally directed and technique-orientated it becomes simply a craft activity.

All the printing ideas in this section would benefit from a brief demonstration to explain and show the activity to the children. Then summarise the main points you want them to remember and put into practice before letting them try things out for themselves.

It's a good idea to remind children about colour-mixing at the start of most printing sessions as this is a useful opportunity to practise this skill (*see* Introduction to Painting, page 38, for more detail). Remind them that with printing, paintbrushes should only be used for mixing paint.

When you do printing with a whole or half class, finding space to dry all the work produced can be a problem. A washing line and pegs are a simple solution to this.

It is easier to get a clear print if the printing table is padded slightly. Several layers of newspaper will help with this.

Basic printing equipment

Depending on activity select from:

● natural printing objects – sections of fruit, vegetables, leaves, potatoes for potato blocks, etc.

● junk printing materials – sponge pieces, carpet pieces, polystyrene packaging, loofah pieces, plastic drinking straws, stiff card, corrugated card, bottle tops, Lego bricks, yogurt pots, pen tops, textured wallpapers, string, wool, bubble wrap, hessian, net, etc.

● sheets of polystyrene cut from trays or from craft suppliers

● Plasticine

● homemade engraving tools – sharpened sticks, knitting needles, etc.

● paints – readymix or thickish powder

● paintbrushes for mixing colours

● flat mixing palettes

● water jars

● water-based printing ink

● oil-based printing ink

● rollers and flat trays

● white spirit if using oil-based ink

● PVA glue and glue spreaders

● small sponges

● sheets of sugar and cartridge paper – variety of colours

● tracing paper

● scrap paper

● coloured pencils

● chalks or pastels

● Formica-covered boards

● clothes line and pegs for drying work

● newspaper to cover and pad work areas

1 Fruit and vegetable prints

Scope
Printing with natural objects

Age
5–6

Organisation
Groups of 6–8

Time
1/2 hour

Cross-curricular links
Science (seasons)

You will need
pieces of firm fruits or vegetables cut across in various sections (citrus fruits, peppers, cauliflower florets, tight white cabbage chunks, apples, carrots, potatoes, etc.); paint in flat trays, either readymix or thickish powder; sugar paper or newsprint

Purpose
● To explore the patterns and shapes that cut sections of fruit and vegetables make when used as printing blocks.

Activity
1 Make the blocks in advance, cutting across the pieces of fruit and vegetables cleanly to give an even cut surface. Chunks are easier to grip if a wedge is cut at either side of the top to make a 'handle'.

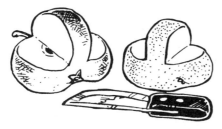

2 Demonstrate printing with the blocks:
– Dip the flat surface of your chosen block into the paint, then press it down on to the paper.
– Print a further time before dipping into the paint again.
3 Let the children try this.
4 Ask the children to print single prints from all the blocks provided.
5 Then show them how to print patterns in rows and let them try this with selected blocks.

Teaching points
▶ Show the children how to wipe the paint-laden blocks against the side of the tray if the prints are smudgy through too much paint clinging to the block.
▶ It's easier to get clear prints if the printing table is padded slightly. Several layers of newspaper will help with this.

Further activities
▶ Printing rows of patterns on cut-out life-size paper tee-shirt shapes. Show the children how overlapping the prints makes different patterns.
▶ Printing borders for display boards.

2 Introducing junk printing

Scope
Junk printing with textured materials

Age
7–11

Organisation
Half to whole class

Time
3/4 hour

You will need
selection of junk printing materials: small pieces of sponge in rough shapes, pieces of carpet of different types, small lumps of polystyrene packaging, pieces of loofah, short pieces of plastic drinking straw, pieces of stiff card and corrugated card; readymix paint in three primary colours plus white; sugar paper, large and small sheets; paintbrushes; flat mixing palettes; water jars

Purpose
● To encourage the children to explore the effects of simple textured materials in junk printing.

Activity
1 Prepare a list of things that you want the children to try to reproduce. Some suggestions are: flames, clouds, foliage, smoke, long grass, a stone wall, a thatched roof, fur, fish scales, thick snow, a feather, a spider's web.
2 Demonstrate printing with some of the materials on a small piece of paper first.
3 Then fold a larger piece of paper three times to make eight sections, open it out and show how to fill each section with one of the required effects. Don't reproduce all the effects, just one or two examples, and challenge the children to make even better ones.
4 Allow the children five printing materials each. Let them try to reproduce the effects you have suggested on their own paper folded in eight sections.

Teaching points
▶ Remind the children how to mix green, orange, purple, brown and pale tones, if they have not done much colour mixing (*see* Introduction to Painting, page 38, for more details).
▶ Stress that a print is made by pressing down on to the paper, and that, for example, using the sponge as a brush is not printing.
▶ Tell the children that you don't expect every square to be totally successful but that they can have several tries at getting the effects they want.
▶ This exercise would make a good introductory activity to any of the following junk printing ideas.

Further activities
▶ Looking at the work with the class to see how different effects have been obtained.
▶ Give each child a piece of fairly stiff card about 8 cm x 3 cm (pieces cut from cereal boxes are fine), one colour of paint in a flat tray and a piece of paper. Challenge them to produce as many different patterns with the card as they can. They can use it straight, bent, folded, curled up. Have some spare pieces of card available. Then give out pieces of corrugated card for them to try out.

3 House or landscape prints

Scope
Pictures using some of the effects tried out in idea 2

Age
7–11

Organisation
Half to whole class

Time
3/4 hour

Cross-curricular links
Geography (houses and homes)

You will need
junk printing materials as in idea 2; readymix paint in three primary colours plus white and black; paintbrushes; flat mixing palettes; water jars; sheets of paper; scrap paper; Plasticine

Purposes
● To explore the effects of simple textured materials in junk printing.
● To use some of the effects tried out in idea 2 to make pictures.

Activity
1 Remind children of effects obtained in idea 2 and show some of these again.
2 Show how the Plasticine can be made into any shape or block that's needed.
3 Allow the children five junk materials each. Ask them to print a picture of a house or landscape, using some of the effects they tried out in idea 2. They can use small pieces of scrap paper to try out effects.

Teaching points
► Remind the children how to mix colours if necessary (*see* Introduction to Painting, page 38).

Further activities
► You might like to show the children works by John Piper, an English artist whose prints often showed scenes which feature buildings.

4 Vase of flowers prints

Scope
Junk printing combined with making stencilled vase

Age
9–11

Organisation
Half to whole class

Time
1 1/2 hours (can be 2 sessions)

Cross-curricular links
Science (seasons)

You will need
vase of dried grasses and seed pods offering a wide variety of shapes and textures, such as honesty, dried wheat, oats, wild grasses, cow parsley, dock, dried flowers such as statice; sugar paper for stencils; junk printing materials as in idea 2; readymix paint in crimson, yellow, royal blue, scarlet and white; paintbrushes; sponges; flat mixing palettes; water jars; A3 sugar paper in a variety of colours; scrap paper or newsprint

Purposes
● To look closely at the different textures of seed pods, grasses and dried flowers and try to reproduce them.
● To try to mix colours that match specific items.
● To cut a simple stencil and use it.

Activity
1 This activity is for older children with some experience of junk printing. Remind them of the techniques described in ideas 2 and 3.
2 Demonstrate how to cut out a symmetrical stencil for the vase from a piece of folded sugar paper:
– Draw the vase on to the folded paper.
– Cut the shape out, retaining the piece with the hole in it. This is the stencil.
3 Ask the children to make their own vase stencils. (It does not matter if the vase is not like the one on display as long as they like the shape they've cut.)
4 Ask them to place their stencils near the bottom of the large sheets of paper, hold them still, then print the vase, using sponge.
5 Using a piece of card held on its side, show the children how to print some stems in the vase.
6 Let them try out some effects of grasses, etc. on their pieces of scrap

paper, then start to print the grasses and seed pods on the picture.
7 Remind the children about how to mi colours (*see*, Introduction to Painting, page 38), then ask them to try to match some of the colours in the vase of flower and grasses. They do not have to reproduce it exactly. They should look a it and try to reproduce some of the effects that they see.

Teaching points
► This activity could be done in two sessions. The stencils could be prepared in advance.
► Tell the children to use the paint thickly. If they water it down, it 'disappears' into the sugar paper as it dries.
► Remind the children to use their 'try out' pieces of paper as they work.
► Talk to the children about contrasts of texture and colour in their work as the session progresses.

Further activities
► You might like to show the children paintings from various periods, such as those by the Impressionists or Odilon Redon, and compare the effects of works done in different media with their own pictures. Discuss what works well for different types of flowers.

5 Printed portraits

Scope
Junk printing

Age
7–11

Organisation
Up to whole class, depending on equipment and space

Time
1 hour

Cross-curricular links
History (Normans, Tudor portraits)

You will need
Junk printing materials including bottle tops, Lego bricks, half yogurt pots to produce set shapes, selection of textured materials such as sponges, lumps of polystyrene, pieces of corrugated card and ordinary card; readymix paint in three primary colours plus white and black; paintbrushes; flat mixing palettes; water jars; sheets of paper; scrap paper

Purpose
● To explore the potential of printing with a wide selection of junk materials.

Activity
1 Ask the children to try out the materials first on scrap paper. If they are to reproduce a portrait, they should try to get some of the effects they will need as they experiment. Remind them of ways they can use a piece of card to get a variety of effects. Share the ideas developed to encourage the less inventive ones. (The children can also use fingers to print with.)
2 The children use these effects to make a printed portrait. (They could either reproduce historic portraits such as people in decorative Tudor dress or Normans in chain-mail; or a portrait from their own observation.)

Further activities
► You could ask the children to create a border around the finished pictures.
► You could look at pictures of the Bayeux Tapestry and ask the children to try to reproduce some of the scenes, including the writing.
► The children could try illustrating fictional characters such as Ted Hughes' Iron Man (*The Iron Man*, Faber).

6 Troll or monster prints

Scope
Junk printing

Age
5–6

Organisation
5 year-olds: groups of 6–8;
6 year-olds: up to half class

Time
3/4 hour

Cross-curricular links
English (stories, language development work)

You will need
junk printing materials as in idea 5; readymix paint in three primary colours plus white and black; paintbrushes; flat mixing palettes; water jars; sheets of paper; scrap paper

Purpose
● To explore the potential of printing with a wide selection of junk materials.

Activity
1 Ask the children to try out the materials on scrap paper first. Suggest that they try to achieve the effects of fur, scales, hair, nails and teeth, etc. Look at these experiments with them before they start their actual picture. Point out interesting effects and ask the children who produced them to say how they obtained them.

2 The children make their prints of trolls or monsters using the effects they tried out. These could be based on stories such as 'The Three Billy Goats Gruff'.

Further activities
► The children could write descriptions of their trolls and where they live, etc.
► They could make a collection of adjectives that could be used to describe the trolls and monsters.
► They could write a class poem about trolls or monsters.

7 Fireworks and bonfires

Scope
Junk printing

Age
6–9 years

Organisation
Small groups to whole class, depending on age and facilities

Time
1 hour

Cross-curricular links
English (written work on bonfire night or Divali)

You will need
junk printing materials as in idea 5; readymix paint in three primary colours plus white and black; paintbrushes; flat mixing palettes; water jars; sheets of dark blue or black paper; scrap paper; cut-up pieces of plastic drinking straws

Purposes
● To explore the potential of printing with a wide selection of junk materials, including textured materials.
● To try to create specific effects needed for the picture.

Activity
1 Talk to the children about some of the different types of fireworks they may have seen and their descriptive names. Make a list of these: golden showers, snowstorms, Catherine wheels, etc. Talk about the bonfire, too, and how the old things being burnt show up darkly against the flames. Show pictures, if you have them, of things on fire.

2 Give out scrap paper first, and get the children to try to create the effects of flames, sparks and various fireworks with some of the junk printing materials. Look at these and share ideas.
3 Then let them print their individual pictures or ask each child to print lots of fireworks and use these, cut out, to create a class picture. Ask a group to print the bonfire.

8 Printed lizards on leaves

Scope
Exploring the effects of camouflage in nature

Age
7–11

Organisation
Half to whole class

Time
1 hour

Cross-curricular links
Science (camouflage in nature), Geography (tropical rainforests)

You will need
interestingly-shaped large leaves; copies of pcm 8 (optional); small junk printing objects; pieces of card; coloured sugar paper; scrap paper; readymix paint in three primary colours plus white and black; paintbrushes; flat mixing palettes; water jars; books showing camouflage in nature

pcm 8 on page 83

Purposes
● To create different patterns and textures, using a selection of small junk objects.
● To experiment with the effects of camouflage.

Activity
1 Discuss camouflage in nature, showing the children some illustrations in nature books.
2 The children draw and cut out lizard shapes, or cut them out from pcm 8.
3 They look at and draw large leaf shapes and cut these out.
4 Explain that you want them to devise an interesting pattern, trying out some on scrap paper first, and then to print this on the lizard and one or more leaf shapes.
5 When these are dry, they mount the lizards on the leaves.

Teaching points
► These could form part of a large class picture.

Further activities
► The children could investigate other examples of camouflage in nature, then devise some further examples of camouflaged small animals or insects mounted on leaves, rocks or bark.

9 Fantasy bird pictures

Scope
Pictures combining printing with junk and small potato blocks cut into feather shapes

Age
6–9

Organisation
Groups ranging from 8 at 6 years to half class at 9 years

Cross-curricular links
Geography (tropical rainforests 8–9 year-olds, 'our visit to the zoo' 6–7 year-olds), English (naming birds and writing about them)

You will need
ready-cut feather-shaped potato blocks; piece of card for each child; junk materials: pieces of plastic drinking straw, sponges of various types, chunks of polystyrene packaging; readymix paint in three primary colours plus crimson and white; paintbrushes; flat mixing palettes; water jars; sheets of paper in a variety of colours; scrap paper

Purpose
● To explore the potential of marks made with junk materials combined with prints of small specially-shaped potato blocks.

Activity
1 Demonstrate printing with a feather-shaped block.

2 Ask the children to print a picture of a colourful fantasy bird using the blocks and junk materials. You may like to show them pictures of tropical birds and talk to them about their variety of plumage first, but remove these before the children start to work as you want them to create fantasy birds.

3 When they are dry, the birds could be cut out and mounted as part of a composite class picture.

Further activities
► Written work, using the birds as starting points: younger children could think up names for their birds and write poems about them. Older children could also name their birds, then invent details of country of origin, habitat, breeding and feeding habits, etc., based on the way real birds are described in nature books.
► Older children could make printed pictures of owls, using the same junk materials and feather blocks. (Show some owl pictures to the children and discuss the particular characteristics of these birds.) Provide large and small feather shapes. They can print a branch and some leaves, too, if there's space around the owl.

10 Flower prints

Scope
Making prints of vases or bunches of flowers, using potato blocks in petal shapes

Age
7–11

Organisation
Whole class, provided facilities available

Time
1 1/2 hours

You will need
vase of colourful daisy-type flowers; pieces of card; paper for stencils; small pieces of sponge; potato blocks cut into petal shapes (provide ready-cut for younger children); readymix paint in three primary colours plus crimson and white; paintbrushes; flat mixing palettes; water jars; sheets of paper in a variety of pale colours; scrap paper

Purposes
● To try to produce specific effects using simple junk printing materials and small potato blocks cut into petal shapes.
● To practise mixing colours that match colours in nature.

Activity
1 Show the children how to cut and print a vase using a paper stencil (*see* idea 4).
2 Demonstrate printing a flower, using the petal-shaped potato blocks and showing how the flowers are built up of layers of petals.
3 Ask the children to look at the colours of the flowers in the vase and remind them how to mix greens, pinks, oranges, purples and browns (*see* Introduction to Painting, page 38).
4 Ask the children to try printing a flower on scrap paper first and to use

scrap paper as they work to try out effects and colours.
5 Demonstrate printing the vase near the bottom of the sheet of paper and printing a few stems in the vase using card.
6 The children print their vases of flowers.

Further activities
► You could look at flower paintings from different ages (for instance Dutch seventeenth-century works, paintings by Impressionists, Van Gogh, Redon, Winifred Nicholson) and compare the effects of the different media used with the effects that you were able to obtain with printing.
► Discuss with the children, whether it would be possible to reproduce all types of flowers with this type of printing.

11 Stencilled shape patterns

Scope
Making a pattern of stencilled shapes, using chalks

Age
7–11

Organisation
Whole class

Time
1 hour

You will need
A4 grey sugar paper for stencils; chalks or pastels; A3 or bigger sugar paper in assorted colours

Purposes
● To introduce the idea of making a simple stencil.
● To explore the patterns that can be made with one simple shape.

Activity
1 Demonstrate how to make a simple stencil (*see* idea 13). The shapes can be torn or cut.
2 Choose a colour for the background. Lay the stencil over the background and, holding it firmly in place, draw chalk marks all around the edge of the hole.

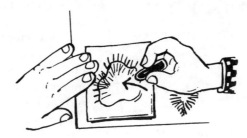

3 Explain that it's important to start each stroke on the stencil itself, and to draw the strokes into the hole, to avoid ripping the stencil.
4 Show the children how to lift the stencil and move it to another part of the paper and repeat the chalking process.
5 Ask them to make their own stencil patterns.
6 Tell them to move their stencils as many times as they like until the pattern seems finished. Get them to try overlapping some patterns. Chalks look effective on bold coloured paper.

Further activities
▶ If the first experiments are done with torn shapes, do the project again with cut shapes.
▶ The children could also try letter shapes and action figure stencils using either chalk or paint sponged on.

12 Stencilled leaf prints

Scope
Stencilled pictures based on leaf shapes

Age
6–11 (activity simple or more complex according to age, *see* Teaching points)

Organisation
Small group to whole class

Time
1 hour, could be 2 sessions

Cross-curricular links
Science (nature study, seasons)

You will need
sugar paper for stencils; medium and large autumn leaves; sponges and other textured printing materials such as pieces of carpet and loofah; readymix paint in three primary colours; paintbrushes; flat mixing palettes; water jars; sheets of sugar paper

Purposes
● To make and use a simple stencil.
● To explore the design potential of various leaf shapes.
● To try out the effects of various printing materials.
● To mix colours.

Activity
1 Demonstrate how to make and print from a leaf stencil (*see* idea 13 for basic method):
– Draw around a leaf on sugar paper and cut this shape out. Cut right into the centre of the shape first, then cut neatly round the shape, leaving a leaf-shaped hole in the middle of the paper.
– Lay this stencil over the chosen background paper and hold it still.
– Mix the colour you want to print with, then sponge this over the stencil. Let some of the texture of the sponge or other printing material show on the print.
2 Let the children make their own leaf stencils and print them.

Teaching points
▶ Choose fairly simple leaf shapes for young children, more complex ones for older ones.
▶ Remind the children that the stencil is the piece of paper with the hole in it!
▶ Older children might be asked to draw their chosen leaf first, and after they have printed the basic shape to print the pattern of veins on the leaf with card.
▶ 10–11 year-olds might be asked to print their leaf several times, overlapping it and noting the effects of different colours on the sections that overlap.

Further activities
▶ Offer a selection of medium and small leaves to 9–11 year-olds and ask them to produce a square tile design based on four prints from their stencil. Tile design squares the same size but different colours could be displayed as a patchwork quilt.
▶ Offer long strips of paper, and ask the children to print a repeat border pattern using only their stencil, a piece of card and their fingers. Let them try out ideas first, before printing a 'best' sample.

13 Stencilled snowmen

Scope
Combining stencilled prints with junk printing

Age
5–7

Organisation
5–6 year-olds: groups of 6; 7 year-olds: larger groups

Time
3/4–1 hour (could be 2 sessions)

Cross-curricular links
Science (winter, weather), English (written work about snow, reading snow poems)

You will need
grey sugar paper for the stencils; junk printing materials: sponges, lumps of polystyrene, pieces of carpet, pieces of card; readymix paint in three primary colours, black and white; paintbrushes; flat mixing palettes; water jars; sheets of sugar paper in black and blue ; scrap paper

Purposes
● To make and use a simple stencil.
● To represent the texture of snow, using junk printing materials.

Activity
1 Demonstrate making a snowman stencil using grey sugar paper:
– Draw the snowman on the paper.
– Cut out the snowman shape, keeping the paper round the snowman in one piece as the stencil.
2 Lay this on the black or blue background paper, then print through the stencil using one of the textured printing materials. Remove the stencil, then print a layer of snow for the snowman to stand on and maybe some snow falling.
3 Ask the children to make their own snowman stencils and snowman pictures.
4 Suggest that they finish off their snowmen by printing eyes, nose, mouth, buttons, etc., using fingers or any of the other bits and pieces that seem appropriate. They can try these out on scrap paper as necessary.

Teaching points
▶ Remind the children that the stencil is the piece of paper with the hole in it!
▶ Talk to them about the texture of the snow, and ask them to try out which printing materials make marks that suggest this texture most effectively.
▶ Tell them that you expect all the snowmen to end up different from each other.

Further activities
▶ Written work about snow, especially its texture.
▶ Read some poems about winter activities to the children.

14 Patterned fish

Scope
Combining stencilled prints with junk printing

Age
7–11 (children who have done some printing)

Organisation
Stencils: whole class; printing: up to half class, depending on facilities

Time
1 1/4 hours (could be 2 sessions)

You will need
A3 grey sugar paper for stencils; junk printing materials, including small sponges, pieces of card; readymix paint in three primary colours plus white; paintbrushes; water jars; flat mixing palettes; sugar paper in pastel shades; scrap paper

Purposes
● To make and use a simple stencil.
● To experiment with the effects that can be obtained from printing with a variety of junk objects.
● To develop some repeat patterns, using simple printing tools.

Activity
1 Demonstrate making a fish stencil (*see* idea 13). The fish should almost fill the A3 paper.
2 Ask the children to choose five or six junk materials to print with, including a small sponge and piece of card each.
3 Ask them to try out their selection of printing materials on scrap paper first, then develop some simple repeat patterns in rows, using some of these effects.
4 The children then lay the stencils on their chosen background paper and print repeat patterns on the fish shape.
5 Suggest they remove the stencil from time to time to see the effect of the whole picture.
6 They could print seaweed, sand, small fish, etc., to finish off the picture.

Teaching points
▶ You may like to make the stencils in advance of the painting part of the lesson.
▶ Remind the children about basic colour mixing as you demonstrate (*see* Introduction to Painting, page 38).
▶ Trying out the printing materials and developing the patterns on scrap paper is an important part of the session.

Further activities
▶ You could try combining a stencil with junk pattern printing on a butterfly. This would have the added complication of printing symmetrical patterns on each wing. It could be linked to work on symmetry.

15 Stencilled Christmas trees

Scope
Combining simple stencils with junk printing

Age
6–10

Organisation
6–8 year-olds: small groups;
9–10 year-olds: whole class

Time
1 hour

Cross-curricular links
RE (Christmas)

You will need
A3 grey sugar paper for the stencils; junk printing materials: textured materials, bottle tops, pen tops, Lego bricks, etc., pieces of card; readymix paint in three primary colours plus white; paintbrushes; water jars; flat mixing palettes; sugar paper in a variety of bold colours ; scrap paper

Purposes
● To make and use a simple stencil.
● To experiment with the effects that can be obtained when printing with a variety of junk objects.

Activity
1 Demonstrate making a Christmas tree stencil (*see* idea 4 for basic method) and printing from it:
– Fold the grey paper in half lengthwise.
– Place this on your chosen background paper and print the tree in green, using a sponge or other textured materials. Then remove the stencil.
2 Ask the children to make and print their own stencilled Christmas trees.
3 Suggest they try to print the effect of lights, candles, gifts, decorations on scrap paper, using any of the junk objects provided.

4 Suggest they print successful ones on the trees, which should have dried a bit by this time.

Teaching points
► Remind younger children how to mix green (*see* idea 55).
► Some children may need help envisaging half a tree. I always ask them to have a go first before helping them. You could use pages of magazine paper for the stencils, in which case it doesn't matter how many goes they have.
► Bold colours of background paper look best for this activity.

Further activities
► The children might simply print the trees, then leave them, decorating them with cut paper work when they are dry.

16 Stencilled animal pictures

Scope
Printed pictures using two stencils

Age
9–11 (children who have done some work with stencils)

Organisation
Half to whole class

Time
1–1 1/2 hours (best done in 2 sessions)

Cross-curricular links
Science (pets)

You will need
A4 white cartridge paper; A4 tracing paper; A4 grey sugar paper; craft knife (optional); sponges and other textured objects; readymix paint in three primary colours plus white and black; paintbrushes; water jars; flat mixing palettes; sheets of paper at least as large as the stencil paper

Purposes
● To design a picture in two colours.
● To make and use two stencils, one for each colour in the design.
● To learn about the need for accuracy with this technique.

Activity
1 Demonstrate making two-colour animal stencil pictures:
– Draw an animal design on white paper.
– Use the tracing paper to trace what will be the main outline of the animal on to the grey paper.
– Cut this out.
– Trace what will be printed in the second colour, such as the features or any other details, on to a second piece of grey paper.
– Cut this out. (Make sure that you get the edges of these stencil sheets accurately registered on top of each other, or the details of the second stencil will not print in the right place over the outline of the animal.)
– Show the children how the stencils fit over each other, if necessary drawing round each one in turn.

– Now demonstrate printing the two stencils with paint, using a sponge.
2 Ask the children to make their own two-colour animal stencils.

Teaching points
► The outline stencil needs to give a lot of information about the animal, so tell the children to choose an animal with a distinctive shape.
► The second stencil could be cut using a craft knife if the details are very fine. You will need to provide strong cartridge paper for this. If you want to avoid fine detail, you could work to A3 size.
► Same size sheets of paper simplify the problem of registering the design accurately.
► If the background sheets and stencil sheets are different sizes, teach the children to mark the corners of the stencil sheet on the background paper. Both stencils need to be the same size.

Further activities
► This project makes a good introduction to screen printing. Other suitable subjects would be a face or mask, a flower, a butterfly or fish.

17 Engraved insect prints

Scope
Insect pictures engraved on a polystyrene block and printed

Age
5–7

Organisation
5–6 year-olds: groups of 6–8;
7 year-olds: up to half class

Time
3/4 hour

Cross-curricular links
Science (mini-beasts)

You will need
small rectangles of polystyrene sheet; readymix paint with a dash of washing-up liquid in 2 or 3 bold colours; brush or sponge; small sheets of white or coloured paper; newspaper for work area

Purpose
● To give the children the experience of printing from an engraved block.

Activity
1 Demonstrate making the block and printing from it:
– Draw a picture of the chosen insect on the surface of the polystyrene, pressing the point of the pencil hard to engrave the image.
– Sponge or paint the surface of the block.
– Lay a piece of paper over the block, then smooth over the top of the paper.
– Peel the paper off the block and show the print to the children. Repeat using a different colour paint.
2 Ask the children to engrave their own

insect blocks and to print from them.

Teaching points
► The print will be a reverse image of the block.
► Laying the paper over the block enables children to get a clearer print than pressing the block on to the paper.
► The washing-up liquid helps paint to adhere to the surface of the polystyrene, but prints could also be made using water-based printing ink and a small rubber roller. This would give clearer prints but is messier to use.

Further activities
► The children could explore the different marks, such as dots, that can be made on the block, and how these print.

18 Engraved leaf prints

Scope
Engraved polystyrene block of a leaf, to be used in several ways

Age
8–11

Organisation
Block-making: up to whole class; printing in pairs in printing area

Time
Block-making: 1/2 hour; printing: 1 hour (could be 2 sessions)

Cross-curricular links
Science (autumn)

You will need
autumn leaves; sheets of polystyrene; stiff card cut from cardboard cartons; glue and glue spreaders; water-based printing ink; rubber rollers and flat trays; sheets of white and pastel coloured paper; newspaper for work area

Purposes
● To look closely at the patterns of veins in a leaf and to draw them.
● To make an engraved printing block and print from it.

Activity
1 Demonstrate making the block and printing from it:
– Place your chosen leaf on the polystyrene and draw round it.
– Cut out the leaf from the polystyrene and stick it on to a rectangle of stiff card.
– Referring to the leaf, engrave the pattern of veins on to the polystyrene leaf with a pencil.
– Allow the glue to dry.
– Squeeze a small amount of printing ink on to the flat tray.
– Spread this with the roller until the roller is evenly coated.
– Roll the ink on to the surface of the block.
– Move the block on to a clean area of newspaper and lay a piece of paper over it.
– Smooth this with your hand, then peel the print off the block.
– Make another print on a different coloured paper.

2 Ask the children to make their own engraved leaf prints.

Teaching points
► You get clearer prints by putting the paper over the block, unless you have access to a printing press.
► Have a good supply of clean newspaper available and teach the children to put clean paper down when the work area becomes inky, or their prints will be messy too.
► Allow only two children in the printing area at a time.

Further activities
► Using the same printing block, challenge the children to design:
(a) a border print on a long strip of paper;
(b) a four-square 'tile' pattern on a square piece of paper;
(c) an all-over design for wrapping paper, seeing the effects of overlapping the leaf prints and sometimes printing without re-inking the block to get paler prints. You may like to show the children examples of tiles, border designs, etc. Repeating patterns like these are best done pressing the block down on to the paper on a slightly padded surface.

19 'Exploded shape' prints

Scope
Engraved printing blocks made from pieces of polystyrene stuck on stiff card

Age
7–10

Organisation
Block-making: up to whole class; printing area: small groups or pairs

Time
Block-making: 1/2 hour; printing: 1 hour (could be 2 sessions)

You will need
sheets of polystyrene; rectangles of stiff card cut from cardboard cartons; glue and glue spreaders; printing ink or readymix paint mixed with a little washing-up liquid; flat trays and rubber rollers or paintbrushes or sponges; sheets of white and pastel coloured paper; newspaper for work area

Purpose
● To make a simple printing block and print from it.

Activity
1 Demonstrate making the block and printing from it:
– Cut a shape from the piece of polystyrene.
– Cut across this shape several times so that it is in about eight fragments.
– Arrange these on a piece of stiff card, then stick them down.
– Allow the blocks to dry. (You might take a **rubbing** of the block at this stage.)
– Show the children how to coat the block, the older ones using printing ink and a roller (*see* idea 18), the younger ones using a sponge or brush and paint.
– Lay a piece of paper over the coated block.

– Smooth over the back of the paper, using your hand, then peel the print off the block.
2 Ask the children to make their own blocks and print their own 'exploded shapes'.

Teaching points
See idea 18.

Further activities
► These blocks could be made more detailed by engraving some of the areas of polystyrene. This might be done after the first prints have been taken, and the children challenged to see what different textures they could devise and engrave into the polystyrene with a pencil or simple tool.

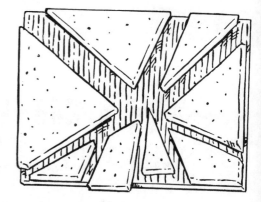

20 Two-colour designs

Scope
Prints from two small blocks, inspired by Japanese woodblock designs

Age
9–11

Organisation
Block-making: up to whole class; printing area: small groups or pairs, depending on equipment available

Time
2 hours in 3 sessions

Cross-curricular links
Geography (culture of Japan)

Purposes
● To look closely at the craftsmanship in Japanese woodblock designs.
● To work out an engraved design based on some motifs in these designs.
● To design two blocks that go together to make a single motif.

Activity
Session 1
1 With the children, look at examples of Japanese woodblock prints. (There are examples in many art packs, or in books on Japanese art.) Try to find examples of simple motifs, such as patterns in clothing. Talk about how these designs were carved into blocks of wood and about the need for the two blocks to fit over each other accurately.
2 Encourage the children to work out their own two-block designs.

Sessions 2 and 3
3 Demonstrate making the two blocks and printing:
– Draw a simple design on paper, using a circular, triangular or other simple shape as the basis of the design.
– Draw the design using lines and dots only.
– Cut out this shape twice in polystyrene.
– Stick the shapes onto card, trimming the card to the size of the polystyrene.
– Leave one of these blocks plain, explaining that this will be used to print the pale background colour of the design.
– Engrave the second block with the design, using a pencil or other sharp tool.
– Now demonstrate printing with the first block, using a pale colour and pressing the block down firmly on to the paper.

– When the first block is dry, overprint it with the second block, using black ink and positioning it carefully on the first. (For the demonstration you could make the first print in advance so it is already dry.)

– When you have done a simple try-out print, you might like to demonstrate using the block in a variety of ways to build up more complex designs.

4 Ask the children to make their own blocks, then print from their first blocks and leave to dry.

5 In session 3 they overprint with the second block in black ink.

Teaching points
▷ Allow about half an hour for the demonstration, then sum up for the children the main points they need to remember for making the blocks.

▷ Remind them before they print about the need for accuracy.

▷ It will be easier to get clear prints if the printing table is slightly padded; even a thick layer of newspaper will help with this.

Further activities
▷ Slightly larger designs printed with oil-based ink on fabric could be used to make bags or cushion covers.

▷ Small leaf shapes or simple geometric shapes such as triangles, diamonds and hexagons, could be used as the basis for the designs.

 # 21 Collagraph prints

Purposes
● To make a **collagraph** block using a variety of different textured materials.
● To observe the effects these give when the prints are taken from the block.
● To use a printing roller and ink.

Activity
Session 1
1 Demonstrate making the collagraph:
– Stick pieces of various textured materials on a sheet of card and leave them to dry.
2 Ask the children to make their own textured blocks, leaving them to dry.
Session 2
3 Demonstrate printing from the collagraph:
– Squeeze a little ink on to the tray and spread this over the tray with the roller until the roller is coated.
– Ink the block and press a sheet of paper on to it.
– Smooth over the back of the paper firmly, then peel the print off the block.

– Repeat this printing process, as the second print, when the block is more thoroughly coated with ink, is often clearer than the first.
4 Ask the children to print from their own textured blocks.

Teaching points
▷ The arrangement of bits and pieces can be fairly random, as the purpose of the activity is to see how the various materials print.

▷ It is a good idea to give the children the opportunity to build on their experience and let them make a second block with a picture or design, using some of the effects it is possible to get.

▷ If you have a printing press, use this as the prints will be clearer.

Further activities
▷ Textured picture blocks could be used to illustrate a variety of topic work, including houses and homes.

22 Shoe sole prints

Scope
Making collagraph prints of shoe soles

Age
7–11

Organisation
Block-making: whole class; printing: small groups or pairs, depending on number of rollers available

Time
Block-making: 1/2 hour; printing: 20 minutes (2 sessions)

You will need
strong card cut from cardboard cartons; textured materials, as for idea 21; PVA glue and glue spreaders; printing ink, water- or oil-based; rollers and flat trays; paper in various colours; newspaper for work area; white spirit if using oil-based ink

Purposes
● To look at patterns in the environment.
● To make a printing block shaped like the sole of a shoe or trainer, using a variety of materials to make the patterns.
● To use a printing roller and ink.

Activity
Session 1
1 Demonstrate making the **collagraph** block:
– Draw a shoe sole on the card, or draw round a shoe.
– Cut this out.
– Make patterns on this, gluing on various textured materials which must be approximately the same thickness.
– Leave the block to dry.
2 Ask the children to make their own shoe sole blocks.

Session 2
3 Demonstrate printing with the block:
– Squeeze a little ink on to the tray and use the roller to spread this over the tray until the roller is coated. Ink the block and press a sheet of paper on to it.

– Smooth over the back of the paper firmly, then peel the print off the block.
– Repeat this process as the second print is often clearer than the first.
4 Ask the children, in small groups or pairs, to print from their blocks.

Teaching points
▶ You may like to look at a variety of shoe and trainer sole patterns with the children before doing this activity, and take rubbings from them.
▶ If using oil-based printing ink, you will need to explain to the children about cleaning with white spirit. Printing with oil-based ink is not as messy as it sounds, especially if you only have one or two rollers and trays and the children take turns to print. The ink dries quite fast and gives good clear prints. But you will need to protect tables and clothes.

Further activities
▶ Looking at patterns in the environment and in nature. Reproducing some of these through drawings, rubbings and more prints.

23 Engraved mono-prints

Scope
Prints taken from designs drawn directly on to an inked surface

Age
7–11

Organisation
Pairs for each roller in printing area

Time
20 minutes printing time

You will need
Formica-covered board about 25 cm by 35 cm or this size work area covered in Formica, marked off with masking tape; A3 paper, white or coloured; rollers and flat trays; printing ink, either water- or oil-based; white spirit, if using oil-based ink; selection of home-made engraving tools, such as sharpened sticks, knitting needles and lolly sticks with the ends cut off straight; newspaper for work area

Purposes
● To introduce the children to a particular technique of printing, giving them time to experiment.
● To give experience of using a roller and printing ink.

Activity
1 Demonstrate making the **mono-print** block and printing from it:
– Squeeze a little ink on to the tray and coat the roller.
– Coat either the Formica-covered board or marked out work area.
– Engrave some patterns on to the surface of the ink, trying out different tools.
– Take a print of your experiments by placing a piece of paper over the surface of the ink, smoothing over the back of the paper with your hands.

– Peel the print off the inked surface.
– Re-ink the printing surface and draw another design on it.
– Make another print.
2 Ask the children to make their own experiments and designs on an inked surface and print from them.

Teaching points
▶ Remind the children that the prints will be reverse images of whatever is drawn on to the ink. This is particularly important if the design incorporates lettering; this would need to be worked out from right to left and with the letters in reverse.
▶ Explain that oil-based ink stains won't wash off. White spirit will be needed to clean them.
▶ Prints from oil-based ink dry more quickly than those from water-based ink.

▶ These also have the advantage that they can be coloured when dry with water-colour paints or inks if you wish, without the printing ink being affected.

▶ You could do this with 5–7 year-olds, using finger paints. Let them spread the paints with their hands or a sponge and use their fingers as well as simple tools.

Further activities

▶ Compare the results from this method of mono-printing with those using the drawn method (*see* idea 24). You might specify that the children draw, for example, the same leaf for both activities.

 # **24** Drawn mono-prints

Scope
Print taken from designs drawn on to paper which are then re-drawn over an inked surface

Age
8–10

Organisation
Drawing: whole class;
printing: pairs in printing area

Time
Drawing: 1/2 hour; 10 minutes printing time per child

You will need
Formica-covered board about 25 cm by 35 cm, or this size work area covered in Formica, marked off with masking tape;
A3 white cartridge paper;
coloured pencils; rollers and flat trays;
printing ink, either water- or oil-based;
white spirit, if using oil-based ink;
newspaper for work area

Purposes

● To introduce the children to a particular technique of printing.

● To give experience of using a printing roller and ink.

Activity

1 Demonstrate making the **mono-print**:

– Have a drawing done ready on a sheet of paper.

– Ink up the board or marked-out printing area (*see* idea 23).

– Lay the paper over this area with the drawing facing up.

– Go over all the lines of the drawing, *trying not to rest on or press down on the surrounding paper as your draw.* Use a coloured pencil for this so that you can see easily which lines you have gone over.

– Peel the print away from the inked surface. The drawn lines will have picked up the ink from the block and will show up as bold lines, the opposite effect to the engraved mono-print method.

– Re-ink the surface ready for the next print.

2 Ask the children to make their own designs and drawn mono-prints.

Teaching points

▶ Remind the children that these prints will be reverse images of their pictures (*see* Teaching points, idea 23).

▶ *See* Teaching points, idea 23 for notes about oil-based and water-based inks.

▶ Drawings of autumn leaves would make good studies for this printing process.

▶ Prints using oil-based inks could be coloured afterwards with watercolours or drawing inks, allowing the colours to flood together.

▶ The hardest part of this printing method is trying not to press down on the surrounding paper as you go over the drawn lines. This is important for obtaining a clear print.

▶ Compare results of this method with idea 23.

25 Marbling paper

Scope
Marbling paper, using oil paints, and ideas for using the papers

Age
6–11

Organisation
Demonstration: whole class 8–11 year-olds, small groups 6–7 year-olds; marbling: pairs of children at sink or tray

Time
10 minutes for each pair

Cross-curricular links
Science (sea or pond projects), Geography (local environment)

You will need
sink or plastic tray with capacity for floating A4 pages, at least; oil paints in two deep, clear colours such as prussian blue, deep cadmium red, cerulean blue; white spirit; jam jar and paintbrush for each colour; stick for stirring; A4 paper, mainly white, some pastel shades; newspaper

Purposes
● To make attractive patterns on paper for use in other art projects.
● To explore another type of printing.

Activity
1 Prepare by filling the tray or sink about half-full of cold water. To one side put a stack of newspaper, the first one opened out ready to receive the first paper. In each jam jar squeeze about an inch of paint. Then pour in some white spirit, about one inch up the jar. Stir well, keeping a separate brush in each jar.
2 Demonstrate **marbling** paper:
– Write your name at the top of two pieces of paper.
– Using the brush that was used for stirring, drop some paint on to the surface of the water in the sink or plastic tray.
– Flick a little of a second colour on to the water.
– Stir this gently until you like the pattern that has formed.
– Gently place a sheet of paper on the surface of the water, keeping the name facing upwards. The paper will pick up the paint immediately.
– Remove the paper straight away and place it on the newspaper.
– Put two layers of newspaper over the top to soak up excess water, then this area will be ready for the next print.
– Take a second print from the remaining paint, which may look very pale on the surface of the water.
3 Let the children, in pairs, make their own marbled papers.

Teaching points
▶ Point out to the children that marbling is a form of printing.
▶ The paint floats on the water because it is oily. Ideally, offer three or four colours of mixed-up paint for the children to choose from, but restrict them to two colours for first experiments.
▶ 6 – 8 year-olds need an adult on hand to supervise this activity.
▶ Modern cleaning materials are very powerful, so wipe out the sink with white spirit before you start work, otherwise residues of the cleaners react with the oil paint.
▶ Marbling inks can be obtained from art suppliers. Follow the instructions on the pack. However, marbling with oil paints as described above is almost foolproof and very economical.

Further activities
▶ The papers can be used for various art projects: for example, blue and green papers make good backgrounds for under-sea collages or 3-D boxes with underwater scenes. (*See* also ideas 45, 47). They also make lovely backgrounds for silhouette pictures cut from black paper. (*See Easter and Christmas* by Jan Pienkowski for inspiring examples of this type of work.)
▶ The papers could be linked to work on the local environment as backgrounds to a silhouette of the local skyline, for example.
▶ The papers might also be used as a background for stencil printing. Save any spare papers for future collage work.

Collage work

See pcm on page 77 for examples of collage techniques

Collage work is making pictures in a variety of materials such as papers, fabrics, natural and man-made materials. The activities in this section offer ideas for working with all of these.

The value of working in collage lies in handling, sorting and selecting from a wide range of patterned and textured materials. Even with paper collage this can be achieved by offering as wide a choice of papers as you can collect.

Paper collage

You may like to consider having a permanent 'paper bit box' for collage activities, full of any interesting papers you can collect to supplement the more ordinary papers available. An interesting selection of papers offers the possibility of an enormous number of contrasts in collage work – in quality of line (torn or cut), shape of pieces, size of pieces, matt/shiny, opaque/transparent, thick/thin, crumpled or textured/flat, patterned/plain, dark/light. These effects will be achieved at an instinctive level in the early years. It is these contrasts which add interest to collage work.

Paper collage work offers five- to seven- year-olds the chance to practise their limited cutting skills and teaches children to tear paper in a controlled way. When teaching tearing skills, I tell the children to 'nibble the paper' with their finger ends. Five- to seven- year-olds could practise the skill by tearing small pieces in random shapes that can be stuck on to cut-out shapes – for instance, torn stripes or patterns could be stuck on to cut-out T-shirt shapes. Being able to tear paper shapes as well as cut them offers the contrast between an interesting, slightly irregular torn outline and a sharp cut line.

Collage in mixed materials

Try to accumulate a wide variety of materials, including junk materials. If you are using fabrics, ideally you need a range of fabrics with varying textures (see below). Perhaps cut up old clothes. Even tiny pieces are useful. Junk materials suggestions for collage are listed below. Again, it is useful to have fabric and junk 'bit boxes'.

Through doing collage in mixed materials, children will experience a great number of contrasts of texture, as well as colour, shape, line and tone. During the early years, their decisions about these elements will be instinctive but nine- to eleven-year olds should be making thoughtful, appropriate and inventive choices from the materials provided.

Collage work, offers the opportunity to consider composition and balance in a piece of work, especially if you emphasise to the children that they should not stick the pieces down straightaway, but collect a number of pieces and try out several arrangements first. This approach works particularly well with eight- to eleven-year olds for symmetrical pattern-making activities.

As emphasised in the general Introduction, remember to remove your sample from view before the children start work.

Although most of the ideas on the following pages offer a highly structured starting point, from within this framework much highly individual work should emerge.

Basic collage equipment

Depending on activity select from:

- papers – sugar, cartridge, tissue, poster or craft, crepe, foil, marbled, wrapping including patterned wrapping, corrugated card, doilies, textured wallpapers, patterned insides of envelopes, manilla envelopes (for flesh-coloured European faces), colour supplements, etc.
- fabrics – rough, smooth, fine, thick, woollen, tweed, silk, net, velvet, satin, fur, etc.
- junk materials – wool, string, raffia, polystyrene trays and packaging shapes, fruit and vegetable nets, foam offcuts, coloured polythene carrier bags, cellophane wrapping, foam packaging, buttons, ribbons, straw, hay, wood shavings, beads, pipe cleaners, pasta shapes, pulses, etc.
- natural materials – leaves, berries twigs
- card
- cotton wool
- glue and glue spreaders
- sheets of sugar and cartridge paper – varieties of colours
- scissors that can cut fabric
- wax crayons
- pastels
- newspapers to glue on
- 'bit boxes'

26 Kaleidoscope patterns

Scope
Torn and cut symmetrical paper collage patterns

Age
8–11 (could be done with 5–7 year-olds if simplified)

Organisation
Individual work in whole class or groups

Time
1–1 1/2 hours

Cross-curricular links
RE (Christmas, Divali or other festivals), Maths (symmetry)

You will need
squares of black and brightly coloured sugar paper, 30 or 40 cm square; variety of different papers approximately A5, including tissue, sugar, craft, foil, marbled, etc; glue and glue spreaders; newspaper to glue on

Purposes
● To practise tearing paper and to explore the use of torn paper shapes.
● To look at the effects of symmetry when making patterns.
● To experience a variety of different paper textures and patterns.
● To make a pleasing composition.

Activity
This is an almost foolproof project, yet one which offers great scope for learning. The activity can be done with torn or cut paper shapes; torn papers produce more interesting shapes.

1 Demonstrate making a symmetrical **collage** pattern:
– Fold the background paper into four square sections, then open it out flat.
– Take a piece of contrasting paper and fold it until you have four layers.
– Tear some shapes out of this. (Tell the children to 'nibble' the paper with their finger ends; then they can control the shapes they tear.)
– Lay one each of these torn shapes in each section of the background paper to make a symmetrical pattern.
– Tear another four shapes out of a different paper and arrange these on the background as well, one in each section.
– Show the children how the pattern alters when you move the pieces round on the background.
– Stick the shapes down when you like the pattern they make.

2 Ask the children to make their own symmetrical collage patterns.

Teaching points
▶ Suggest that the children tear out several pieces and arrange them without sticking them down, so that they can alter the arrangement and consider the patterns that emerge. (Ask them to consider contrasts of colour, shape and size of the pieces they tear and use.)
▶ Sometimes the 'offcuts' make interesting shapes. Suggest they consider using these too.
▶ Placing pieces on top or overlapping others adds depth to the work.
▶ Some children might like to introduce 3-D elements into their work, such as folded concertinas of paper, spirals or curled paper. (They usually come up with their own ideas.)
▶ Have a break after half an hour or so and let the children look round at what other people are doing. Encourage them to share discoveries and ideas.
▶ Small bits of foil add a festive air to the patterns. Tiny pieces add detail.

Further activities
▶ 10–11 year-olds may like to do a more complex version of this project on hexagonal pieces of paper. These could be based on views through a real kaleidoscope and would end up as three mirror image patterns forming one pattern.
▶ 6–7 year-olds could do a pattern based on a single fold, tearing two pieces from folded paper, and placing them opposite each other on the background.

27 Paper collage butterflies

Scope
Torn symmetrical paper collage patterns on large cut-out butterfly shapes

Age
5–7

Organisation
Whole class (butterfly shapes cut in advance), or groups

Time
1 hour

Cross-curricular links
Science (life-cycle of butterflies)

Purposes
● To practise tearing paper and to explore the use of torn paper shapes.
● To create a symmetrical pattern.
● To experience a wide variety of different paper textures and patterns.

Activity
1 With the children, look at pictures of butterflies and talk about the symmetry of patterns on the wings.
2 Demonstrate making symmetrical **collage** butterflies:

– Show the children the butterfly shape, opened out.
– Fold a piece of contrasting paper in half and tear a shape out, producing two symmetrical shapes.
– Place one shape on each butterfly wing.
– Tear some more shapes out and arrange them on the wings too.
– Move the pieces around, then stick them down when you're happy with the symmetrical arrangement.

3 To make 3-D bodies for the butterflies:
– Roll the cardboard tubes in black paper and tuck the ends into the tube.
– Attach a bent pipe cleaner to one end to form antennae.
– Stick the butterfly on to the tube and leave to dry.
4 Ask the children to make their own butterflies.

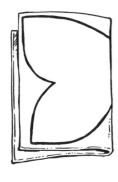

Teaching points
▶ Teach the children to 'nibble' at the paper with their fingers (*see* idea 26).
▶ Remind the children to try to position the torn pieces so that the finished butterfly will be symmetrical.
▶ Suggest that they tear some large shapes and some small ones.
▶ You may like to provide scissors, too, so that the children can introduce cut shapes into their work.

Further activities
▶ This activity could be done on a smaller scale with children aged 9–11 as part of a rainforest project. You could provide photographs of real varieties of butterfly for the children to reproduce or ask them to design their own.

28 Mr and Mrs Autumn

Purposes
● To look closely at the different leaf shapes and the patterns that the veins make.
● To practise cutting out simple and complex shapes.

Activity
1 Demonstrate making leaf **rubbings**:
– Lay a leaf under a piece of pastel coloured paper, holding it down with one hand while crayoning firmly on the paper over half the leaf, until the pattern of the leaf appears.
– Now move your hand and crayon over the other half of the leaf.
– Cut this out.
2 Ask the children to make their own leaf rubbings.
3 Organise some children to mark out and cut out a large shape of a person. (The easiest way to do this would be to draw around someone who is lying on the paper.)

4 Suggest to the children that they stick their leaves on the cut-out person, starting at the hands and feet and working up the body so that the leaves overlap each other like feathers on a bird.
5 You could give a small group the face to do, and suggest that the leaves for the features might be either 3-D or done on a bolder coloured background so that the features show up well.

Teaching points
▶ Ask the children to look at the pattern that the veins of each leaf make.

Further activities
▶ Children could do individual or group projects using cut-out leaf rubbings. They could be provided with background paper and asked to make a pattern or arrangement, using their leaves.

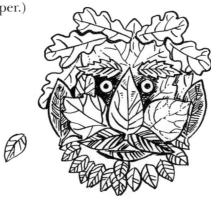

29 Christmas tree collages

Scope
Torn paper collage work on cut-out tree shapes

Age
5–7

Organisation
Individual work in groups or whole class

Time
1 hour

Cross-curricular links
Maths (symmetry), RE (Christmas)

You will need
A3 paper in a variety of colours; cut-out Christmas tree shapes in green paper; glue and glue spreaders; variety of different papers, including small pieces of foil paper; newspaper to glue on

Purposes
● To provide practise in tearing paper in a controlled way.
● To create a symmetrical pattern.
● To experience a wide variety of different paper textures and patterns.

Activity
1 Demonstrate making a Christmas tree **collage**:
– Stick a Christmas tree shape on to background paper.
– Fold a small piece of paper in half, then tear out a shape.
– Place one shape on each side of the tree.
– Tear out some more small shapes from folded paper.

– Arrange these symmetrically on the tree.
– Stick them on when you like the pattern they make.
2 Ask the children to make their own Christmas tree collages.

Teaching points
► Teach the children to tear paper in a controlled way (*see* idea 26).
► Tell them that these are patterned trees and that you do not want representations of presents, toys, etc.
► The children may like to include some simple 3-D bits such as crumpled paper balls in their work.

30 Vase of flowers collages

Scope
Paper collage based on observation of real flowers in season

Age
8–11, possibly 7 year-olds as a group project

Organisation
Individual work in groups or whole class

Time
1 1/2 hours

Cross-curricular links
Science (seasons)

Purposes
● To look closely at the colours and forms of various flowers.
● To reproduce them in suitable papers.

Activity
1 Look at the flowers with the children, and talk about their essential quantities – for instance, dahlias have many layers of petals; some have pointed, some more rounded petals; they come in rich, bright colours and are mostly big and bold.
2 Demonstrate making a vase of flowers **collage**:
– Make a flower shape from a piece of paper folded into four layers (*see* pcm 30 for patterns). Make several of these and place them over each other to build up the layers.
– Stick them together with a dab of glue in the centre.
– Cut a symmetrical vase from a piece of folded paper.
– Mount this on background paper.

– Draw some stems coming out of the vase.
– Arrange several flowers on the stems until you like the shape that they make.
3 Ask the children to make their own vase of flowers collages.

Teaching points

► You could ask the children to draw the flowers first, especially with a variety of spring flowers of different types.

► If you do use spring flowers, discuss with the children how they might achieve the effects of, for instance, grape hyacinths, in paper.

► You could suggest the children invent flowers, making this a quite variable activity.

Further activities

► With 9–11 year-olds, instead of looking at real flowers, you could look at Van Gogh's 'Sunflowers' and ask the children to reproduce it as a group project. (Pcm 30 shows how to make one form of sunflower.) Perhaps the whole class could make a first flower from pcm 30, then adapt the idea to copy more closely the variety of flowers in Van Gogh's work. You will need to collect some unusual colours for this collage.

31 Urn of flowers

Purposes

● To look at an example of a Dutch Master flower painting and reproduce the feeling of abundance that it suggests.

● With older, more experienced children, to reproduce the paintings more accurately.

Activity

1 With the children, look at a copy of a Dutch Master flower painting, such as 'Fruit and Flowers in a Terracotta Vase' by Jan Van Os. (This well-known work is often reproduced as a sheet of wrapping paper large enough to look at with a whole class.) Talk about the work with the class, allowing each child to say one thing that they notice. There's lots to look at!

2 Demonstrate making flowers for the arrangement:

– Use a circle of tissue paper folded into quarters for daisy-type flowers.

– Draw some petals on the folded circle, using the pattern on pcm 31 and cut these out.

– Open out the circle.

– Cut another layer in the same or contrasting colour and stick this on the first layer, using a dab of glue in the centre.

– Make a centre for the flower, flat or 3-D.

– You could make flowers from petals that have been cut from a folded strip of paper, too, sticking these round the edge of a small circle of paper.

– Show the children how to make a leaf **rubbing** and cut this out.

3 You will need flowers of all shapes and sizes to add variety to the **collage**, so challenge the children to invent some of the own after looking once more at the original picture.

4 Cut out, or ask some children to cut out, a large symmetrical urn from a folded piece of orange sugar paper.

5 Ask one or two of the children to draw patterns on the urn in orange wax crayons to give an effect similar to the terracotta vase in the Van Os painting.

6 Glue the urn near the foot of the background paper.

7 Tell children to arrange their flowers on the picture as they like, if possible without sticking them down straight away. (You could do this by having the picture laid out on the floor.) Discuss with them what looks right in each position.

8 Discuss what else the picture needs. The children could add leaves and other details such as insects, small butterflies, etc.

Further activities

► You could divide the class into four groups and ask each group to make a picture representing one of the four seasons. You would need to discuss with them what leaves, fruits, flowers, etc., were appropriate to each time of the year.

► You could adapt the original idea to make a harvest picture of autumn leaves, berries, fruits, etc.

32 Pot of geraniums collages

Scope
Collage done after observing or drawing a geranium in a pot

Age
9–11

Organisation
Preliminary drawings: whole class; collages: individual work in whole class or groups

Time
Drawing: 1 hour; collages: 1 1/2 hours

Cross-curricular links
Science (observation of plant formation)

You will need
selection of green papers: tissue, sugar paper, foil paper, craft paper, etc.; green plastic carrier bags; red and pink papers; white, grey or black paper, A3 or larger; brown sugar, tissue and wrapping paper; orange sugar paper for flower pots; glue and glue spreaders; wax crayons; newspapers to glue on

Purposes
● To observe the character of a plant through observational drawing.
● To interpret this more freely in a variety of materials.

Activity
1 With the children, look at a pot of geraniums and ask them to draw either the whole plant or the leaves and flowers.
2 If you don't want the children to draw the plant, a discussion is essential: refer to the way the leaves overlap each other and most of the flower stem rises above the leaves, the way the flowers are in groups, the rounded shape of the leaves and petals, the strong contrast of colour between the flowers and the leaves.
3 Demonstrate making the pot of geraniums **collage**:
– Cut a symmetrical pot from a folded piece of orange sugar paper and stick this near the bottom of the background paper.
– Twist some stems from brown tissue, sugar or wrapping paper and arrange these as if they were growing out of the pot, or draw some stems with wax crayons.

– Tear some leaves from paper, cut some from plastic and arrange these on the stems.
4 Ask the children to make their own pot of geraniums collage.

Teaching points
▶ Remind the children to look at the plant from time to time to see the way it grows.
▶ Remind them how to cut several petals at once from layers of paper.
▶ The collages could have a 3-D look if the leaves were not stuck down flat.
▶ Show how the leaves might be folded to indicate the veins or suggest that the veins might be drawn in with wax crayons.
▶ Tell the children that they don't have to reproduce the plant exactly but that you'd like them to capture its essential qualities.

Further activities
▶ Use a vase of leaves and berries as a starting point for the collages. You might provide extra, loose leaves, and allow the children to make leaf rubbings to use for the collages.

33 Autumn leaf pictures

Scope
Collage pictures made from cut-out paper leaves

Age
7–11, possibly 6 year-olds as class project (*see* Further activities)

Organisation
Individual work in whole class or groups

Time
1 1/2 hours

Cross-curricular links
Science (autumn)

You will need
selection of varied autumn leaves; variety of papers in autumn tints; large sheets of paper for backgrounds – grey, black and deep blue; glue and glue spreaders; pastels or wax crayons; newspapers to glue on

Purposes
● To look at the shapes and tints of autumn leaves.
● To build up a pleasing composition using cut-out paper leaves.

Activity
1 With the children, look at the variety of shapes and colours of autumn leaves and talk about them: point out the pattern that the veins make on the leaf, and show that this is not symmetrical.
2 Discuss animals that hibernate.
3 Demonstrate making an autumn leaf picture:
– Using a leaf as a template, draw round it and cut it out.
– Draw the veins on the leaf, using the actual leaf to observe the pattern they make.

– Have a few leaves ready cut in advance and arrange these in a pleasing way at the bottom of the background paper as if they had fallen there. Stick them down.
– Draw an animal hibernating among the leaves and a background, if you like.
4 Ask the children to make their own autumn leaf pictures.

Teaching points
▶ Tell the children not to stick the leaves down immediately. Suggest that they assemble a collection of cut-out leaves, arrange these until they like the look of the pattern they make and only then stick them down.
▶ Pastel works well with this collage for the drawn part of the work.

Further activities

▶ Leaves could be arranged in patterns rather than as pictures. This could be undertaken as a group of class activity – for example, you could build up a shape grading the colour carefully. Involve the children in the positioning of the leaves.

▶ You might like to show the class examples of the work of Andy Goldsworthy, an environmental artist who uses natural materials, including leaves, to create works of art out-of-doors. Look in art packs for examples, such as the *Primary Art Pictures Resources Pack* (Oliver and Boyd).

34 Leaf patterns

Scope
Regular patterns made using real leaves as templates

Age
7–11 (could be simplified for 5–7 year-olds – *see* Teaching points)

Organisation
Individual work in whole class or groups

Time
1 hour

Cross-curricular links
Science (seasons), Maths (symmetry)

You will need
selection of small and medium-sized leaves with interesting outlines, fresh or pressed; variety of coloured papers; colour supplements for older children (optional); background papers approximately 30 cm square; glue and glue spreaders; newspaper to glue on

Purpose

● To explore composition, looking at shapes and negative shapes made within a regular outline.

Activity

1 Demonstrate making a leaf pattern:
– Fold a piece of paper into four layers, lay a leaf on it and draw round it.
– Cut out the shape so that you have four identical leaves.
– Lay these on a square of background paper and arrange them until you like the pattern they make.
– Arrange them in several ways to show how different the patterns can be.
– Now choose a different leaf and repeat the process, arranging these with the others on the square background paper.

2 Ask the children to make their own leaf patterns.

Teaching points

▶ The leaves can overlap each other.
▶ Veins can be added by drawing or doing **rubbings**.

▶ Stalks or berries can be added, too, depending on what the patterns seem to need to finish them off.

▶ Tell the children not to stick the leaves down immediately, but to try several arrangements first.

▶ Contrasts in size of leaves add interest to the patterns.

▶ If these are all done on the same sized background papers they can be joined together and displayed as a 'quilt'.

▶ 6–7 year-olds might manage this project if they can cut out accurately. 5–6 year-olds could tear and cut pieces of paper in tones of a chosen colour and stick these on to large cut-out leaf shapes. These could then be arranged in symmetrical patterns on larger squares of background paper as a group project.

Further activities

▶ You could do a similar project on long strips of paper and challenge the children to develop a repeating pattern.

35 Paper collage faces

Scope
Stylised faces in black and white on coloured backgrounds

Age
9–11

Organisation
Individual work, half to whole class

Time
1–1 1/2 hours

Cross-curricular links
Geography (art of other cultures – Africa, South America)

You will need
sheets of white and black paper, approximately A4;
sheets of boldly coloured paper for backgrounds, A3 or larger;
glue and glue spreaders;
newspaper to glue on; books showing masks from other cultures

Purposes

● To explore the potential of 3-D paperwork.

● To look at stylised masks and faces in art from another culture.

Activity

1 With the children, look at pictures of decorative masks in books. Discuss how they are stylised, not naturalistic, versions of the human face and can be very decorative.

2 Demonstrate making a **collage** face:

– Fold a piece of paper in half and cut a nose on the fold so that both sides are the same.

– Stick this down at the edges only so that the nose sticks out in 3-D.

– Cut or tear a mouth from folded paper.

– Fold the paper in half and cut or tear two shapes for eyes, ears and eyebrows and stick these down too.

– Look at some of the offcuts from tearing or cutting the features and use any decorative pieces for filling the spaces on the mask in an attractive way.

– You could add some more 3-D effects: ask the children for suggestions and demonstrate some of these for the benefit of the less confident (spirals, folded concertinas and fans, curled paper).

3 Ask the children to make their own paper collage masks or faces.

Teaching points

▶ If the children keep the features near the centre of the background paper it could be rolled into a large tube for a more 3-D effect.

▶ Tell the children that they can add anything they like to the faces and that they don't have to be symmetrical (unless you want this also to be an exercise in symmetry).

Further activities

▶ With 9–11 year-olds you might make faces on which the features are primarily white one side and black the other. For this they will need to cut everything from sheets of white and black paper laid on top of each other, including a half face, an eye, an eyebrow, half a mouth and nose, etc.

36 Plates of food

Scope
Collage exploring a wide range of materials to recreate a variety of textures

Age
7–11 (may also be done with groups of 6 year-old children)

Organisation
Whole class, working individually

Time
1 1/2 hours

Cross-curricular links
Science (food), English

You will need
wide range of collage and junk materials (see Introduction to Collage work, p.21); cardboard cut from brown cartons; scissors that cut fabric; PVA glue and glue spreaders; paper plate for each child; coloured sugar paper; silver paper; newspaper to glue on

Purpose

● To offer the children the opportunity to explore as wide a range of textured materials as possible.

Activity

1 With children used to thinking through art projects for themselves, talk about the idea of a plate of food collage, showing them the range of materials you have assembled and discussing them: ask, for example, what the cotton wool might represent (mashed potato, cream on a dessert, also useful for stuffing 3-D objects). Stress that you're concentrating on textures as well as colour, and that 3-D work will add excitement to the finished dinners, desserts, etc.

2 For less experienced children you might demonstrate assembling a simple plate such as fried egg, chips and beans, and through discussion elicit suggestions for what other materials suggest to the children. Place your polystyrene egg, corrugated card crinkle chips and rolled tissue paper beans on a paper plate to show them the effect, then remove them or some children will immediately try to copy your plate.

3 Stress that you're looking for originality, and want the children to make a colourful, visually interesting meal on a plate.

4 Ask the children to make their own meal on a plate.

5 Halfway through the session demonstrate mounting the plates on a coloured sugar paper mat and adding a silver paper knife and fork, too. (These are quite hard to do, so take some cutlery for the children to look at.)

6 You may like to ask the children to finish off the meals with a dessert on a small paper plate or dish.

Teaching points

▶ Ask the children to try to introduce contrasts of colour and texture to the plates of food. Provide sugar paper in various colour for background mats and encourage the children to see which colour background sets off their finished dinners best. (Follow this up, if there's an opportunity, with discussion on colour theory with 10–11 year-olds.)

▶ Many children struggle with ideas for desserts, possibly due to modern diet, and you may need to make suggestions, for instance: fruit salad, ice cream (cotton wool balls wrapped in thin polythene or tissue paper), cakes and biscuits, sponge pudding.

▶ Encourage the children to try to draw cutlery freehand, after looking at some. If they're really struggling, allow them to draw round some. If you don't have silver paper, use grey paper.

▶ The project can be approached in two different ways: you might ask the children to recreate a specific meal, such as 'my favourite dinner' and find materials to recreate it, or you might invite them to look through the materials and see what foods the materials suggest to them. Whichever approach you decide to take, bear in mind that, from an artistic point of view, collage is about the different and contrasting textures as well as colours, and bring this into your discussion with the children as they work. Sample questions to ask when looking at the finished works:
– Who's done something unusual or clever with the materials?
– Which plate has a great variety of textures on it?
– Who's managed to get a really 3-D look to theirs? How have they done this?
– Which one looks realistic enough to eat?
– Has anyone decorated their plate in an effective way?
Allow several answers to each question. This type of questioning focuses the children's attention on various aspects of the finished work. Only allow the children to answer the specific questions posed, and only allow them to tell you which one they like the best (and they must say what they particularly like about it) at the end of the question and answer session.

Further activities

▶ You might suggest making fantasy 'space dinners' or a dinner for a witch or wizard, if you are doing English work that would link with these ideas.

37 Collage people

Scope
Pictures of people made from a wide variety of collage materials

Age
7–11

Organisation
Individual work in whole class, if space

Time
1 hour

Cross-curricular links
PSE (myself), History (Romans, Egyptians, Vikings)

You will need
collage materials: papers and fabrics, wool, bits and pieces such as buttons, ribbon, paper doilies, etc.; glue and glue spreaders; sugar paper in various colours; flesh-toned papers for faces – range of suitable colours; newspaper to glue on; history books for reference (optional)

Purpose
● To handle and make pictures with a wide variety of **collage** materials.

Activity
1 With the children, look at illustrations in history books of the relevant period, if relating this work to a history project.
2 Talk to the children about the materials you have collected and ask for suggestions about how they might represent hair, for example, or what a certain fabric might be useful for.
3 Ask the children to make their own **collages** of people.

Teaching points
► Encourage the children to be adventurous in their choice of materials.
► Remind them that if they don't stick everything down immediately, it's easy to alter a collage.
► Suggest they try some 3-D effects. Tissue paper can be folded to represent material for a toga, for instance.

38 Most amazing hat collage

Scope
Fantasy pictures in a variety of materials

Age
6–11

Organisation
Individual work in whole class or groups

Time
1 1/2 hours

You will need
collage materials: papers and fabrics, wool, bits and pieces such as feathers, paper doilies, polystyrene packaging shapes, etc.; glue and glue spreaders; sugar paper in various colours; flesh-toned papers for faces – range of suitable colours; newspaper to glue on

Purpose
● To offer the opportunity to handle and make pictures with a wide range of **collage** materials.

Activity
1 Tell the children this is a fancy hat competition. Talk about cutting out a face shape to begin with; about the idea of an amazing hat which could have *anything* on it – from a bowl of fruit to the Empire State building! Or it might just be an unusual and elaborately decorated hat. Discuss a few ideas if you think they need it.

2 Ask the children to make their own hat collages.

Teaching points
► Encourage the children to try out anything they like. It's a chance to have fun and to try out some really unusual ideas for once in a totally free way.
► You might put the collages up, number them and let the children vote for the most unusual hat. Ask them to mark for originality of ideas and the way the materials have been used.

39 Vegetable collages

Scope
Recreating the textures and colours of a vegetable still life

Age
6–11

Organisation
Individual or group collages, whole class or groups

Time
1–1 1/2 hours

Cross-curricular links
Science (harvest)

You will need
vegetable still life (*see* Activity);
collage materials: papers and fabrics, wool, etc.;
glue and glue spreaders;
sugar paper for backgrounds;
newspaper to glue on

Purpose
● To observe the colours and textures of a still life of vegetables and to represent these, using a wide selection of **collage** materials.

Activity
1 Set up a still life of various vegetables. Try to include some with interesting textures such as broccoli, cress and cauliflower, as well as a variety of different shapes and forms. Arrange these against a plain or almost plain background of paper or draped cloth.
2 Look at the still life with the children. Talk to them about how they might represent some of the textures and forms. Their versions can be as flat or 3-D as they like. Demonstrate some of their suggestions for the class to see.

3 Ask the children to make their own vegetable collages, either individually or in groups.

Teaching points
► It's up to you how much realism you ask of the children. You might ask them to focus on the shapes and colours, or you might want them to concentrate on the textures. With 9–11 year-olds you might ask them to draw studies of the arrangement first, then compare the end results and discuss what each medium has to offer.
► This activity would make an attractive display at harvest time.

Further activities
► You might look at reproductions of painted still lifes of fruit and vegetables such as those of the Dutch Masters and compare what the different mediums have to offer.
► You could set up a display of fruits, instead of vegetables.
► This would make an interesting subject for a sewn collage project.

40 Animal collages

Scope
Collage animal pictures in mixed materials and fur fabric

Age
8–11

Organisation
Individual work in whole class or groups

Time
1–1 1/2 hours

Cross-curricular links
Science (animals, pets)

You will need
collage materials: fake-fur fabric (small, cheap pieces), other fabrics and papers;
scissors that cut fabric;
chalk to mark out shapes on fur fabric;
glue and glue spreaders;
sugar paper for backgrounds;
newspaper to glue on;
animal books for reference

Purpose
● To create pictures from a variety of textured collage materials.

Activity
1 With the children, look at pictures of animals.
2 You could ask the children first to draw the animal that they would like to do a **collage** of and show it to you, so that you could see if you have suitable materials among fabrics you have accumulated, including the fur fabric.
3 Demonstrate drawing the shape of an animal's body on the back of the fur fabric. Show that when cut out, the furry side will be a reverse shape from the one you drew. One way of overcoming this is to draw on tracing paper and then to turn the design over, so that the design is reversed on the back of the fabric, the

right way round on the furry side.
4 Ask the children to make their own animal collages.

Teaching points
► Suggest the children arrange a few shapes on the background without sticking them down until they are happy with the look of their picture or have decided what to put behind the animal shape.
► Some children may need help cutting the fur fabric, especially with some school scissors!

Further activities
► This would make a good sewn collage project for top juniors. The children either draw their designs first or make a design in paper collage and make a tracing of this.

41 Scarecrow collages

Scope
Pictures inspired by a poem, made from a wide variety of collage materials

Age
6–11

Organisation
Individual work in whole class or groups

Time
1–1 1/2 hours

Cross-curricular links
English (poem 'The Scarecrow' by James Reeves)

You will need
collage materials: fabrics and papers, wool and buttons, hay, straw or wood shavings; scissors that cut fabric; PVA glue and glue spreaders; sugar paper for backgrounds; pastels or wax crayons (optional); newspaper to glue on

Purposes
● To listen to or read a poem and to try to create the feeling of the poem in a piece of artwork.
● To explore a wide range of papers and fabrics.

Activity
1 Read 'The Scarecrow' by James Reeves to the class. (It is included in several anthologies, including *I like this poem*, Puffin.)
2 Show the children the **collage** materials you have available and talk about what they might be used for to make a scarecrow collage.
3 Ask the children to make their own scarecrow collages.

Teaching points
▶ Once the scarecrow collages are nearly completed, talk to the children about how small details add interest and

contrast: could the scarecrows have a mouse peeping out of their pockets? Would they have patches on their clothes and bits of straw sticking out from their cuffs? (Use twists of tissue paper or wool if no straw is available or you can't face the mess it makes.) Would the children like to cut out their scarecrows, or make a background? What would be an effective way to do this? It could be collage, or drawn with wax crayons or pastels. What is growing in the field that their scarecrow is protecting? Plenty of room for discussion here, especially with town children!

Further activities
▶ Use other poems as starting points for art work. 'The Marrog' by R.C.Scriven in *I like this poem*, ed. Kay Webb (Puffin), would make a good starting point for individual or group collages.

42 Henry the Eighth

Scope
Group collage reproducing a work of art

Age
9–11

Organisation
Group collages, groups of 3 or 4

Time
2 hours or more, depending on size of collage

Cross-curricular links
History (Tudors)

You will need
collage materials: range of fabrics, including rich looking ones such as velvet and satin, variety of papers, wool, paper doilies, gold paper or gold doilies, buttons and beads; scissors that cut fabric; PVA glue and glue spreaders; sugar paper for backgrounds; flesh-coloured paper; newspaper to glue on; books, pictures showing Henry VIII

Purposes
● To look at, discuss and recreate a work of art in collage, paying particular attention to textures.
● To try to create textures in paper, fabrics and other available materials.
● To study the costume of another era.

Activity
1 With the children, look at a reproduction painting of King Henry the Eighth. Let each child in the class tell you one thing that they notice about the work. (They will notice lots of detail in this way.) Talk about the richness of the fabrics depicted and show the fabrics you have available. Talk about the style of dress shown in the portrait.
2 Ask the children to make their Henry the Eighth **collages** in groups of three or four.

Teaching points
▶ Suggest that one or two children draw a simple outline (no detail) of the figure,

so that the group has something to start from.
▶ They will need the portrait to refer to all the time they are working.
▶ Allow them to start tackling the activity themselves, especially if they are used to working in groups, but be available to help.
▶ As the work progresses, discuss the best ways of reproducing the detail on the costume.
▶ Decide in advance how much freedom of interpretation you're going to allow; this may depend on what materials you've managed to collect.
▶ Discuss with the group the best way to do the background.

Further activities
▶ Groups might tackle different historical figures, referring to portraits, such as Queen Elizabeth the First or other Tudor Monarchs.

43 Tropical storm with tiger

Scope
Group collage work based on Henri Rousseau's painting 'Tropical Storm with Tiger'

Age
6–11

Organisation
Group collage, groups of 3 or 4

Time
1 1/2 hours

Cross-curricular links
Science (weather, storms)

You will need
collage materials: range of papers and fabrics, scraps of fur fabric if possible, green polythene carrier bags for foliage, wool and raffia; scissors that cut fabric; glue and glue spreaders; large sheets of sugar paper for background; pastels or crayons ; newspaper to glue on; books on Henri Rousseau showing 'Tropical Storm with Tiger' or *Primary Art Picture Resources Pack* (Oliver and Boyd)

Purposes

● To study a painting and reproduce the work or the spirit of the work in another medium.

● To have the opportunity to handle and use appropriately a wide range of **collage** materials.

Activity

1 Look at a reproduction of Rousseau's painting 'Tropical Storm with Tiger', with the group or whole class. Talk about the different forms of trees and foliage and the different shades of green. (Rousseau said that he used 22 shades of green in this work!) You might look at actual plants or leaves too. Rousseau created the atmosphere of the jungle – crowded and exotic plants, unusual flowers, etc. – without ever having seen it. Ask, *How did he do it? How has he depicted the rain lashing down?* You could look at pictures of other jungle animals as well, if you want a free approach.

2 Define what approach you want the children to take. This could be to reproduce the painting as closely as possible, using appropriate materials; or you might ask them to create their own jungle scene with a particular atmosphere and perhaps a different animal.

3 Ask the children to make their collages, in groups of three or four.

Teaching points

▶ The collage can have 3-D elements.

▶ You could demonstrate cutting out leaves from several layers of tissue paper at once, and remind the children how to make paper flowers (*see* ideas 30, 31 and related pcm).

▶ Talk to the children about choosing an appropriate colour paper for the background and using pastels or crayons on it.

▶ 'Tropical Storm with Tiger' will be found in most books on Henri Rousseau, and is also included in Oliver and Boyd's *Primary Art Picture Resources Pack.*

Further activities

▶ Groups could be asked to interpret the painting in different ways: for example, you might ask one group to concentrate on the various greens, another to concentrate on contrasting textures and another to reproduce the work with a totally different atmosphere and weather. A fourth group could be challenged to make their work as 3-D as possible. (These suggestions are most appropriate for 9–11 year-olds.)

▶ Many works of art lend themselves to this way of working; for example, a Lowry townscape. Layers of houses and scenery can be built up in paper collage. You will need to talk to the children about scale and how the buildings, etc., in the background are smaller and lighter in colour than those in the foreground.

44 Rainforest collage

Scope
Whole class collage mural that can be added to over several weeks

Age
7–11

Organisation
Whole class or groups, group activity

Time
2 hours to start with

Cross-curricular links
Geography (rainforest, South America)

You will need
collage materials: range of papers, fabrics and other textured materials such as corrugated card, polythene bags, wool, raffia, pipe cleaners; scissors which cut fabric; glue and glue spreaders; large sheets of sugar or poster paper joined together or stapled to large notice board for background; house plants; leaves; newspaper to glue on; books showing flora and fauna of the rainforest

Purposes
● To handle and use a wide variety of papers and fabrics.
● To look at various leaf shapes and reproduce them.
● To create patterned birds, butterflies, insects and plant life of another climate.

Activity
1 With the children, look at and talk about pictures showing the variety of leaves, flowers, birds and insects found in the rainforest. You might also look at house plants to study leaf shapes, as these are most often tropical plants. Provide, too, some indigenous leaves for the children to look at and draw round.
2 Demonstrate how to cut out several leaves at once from folded paper (*see* idea 34); how to make flowers (*see* ideas 30, 31and related pcm); how to make butterflies, encouraging the children to look at the patterns on real species; how to make rubbings from bark, etc. to use for tree trunks (*see* idea 28 for how to make rubbings). Don't do all these at once!

3 Work with the class to create the basic scene of trees, creepers and plants, which will be the backdrop.
4 The children then add to the scene over the weeks. Challenge them to create insects, birds, reptiles, other types of flowers, etc. to go on the basic scene. Ask them to look at pictures in books and to create something *in the spirit* of those they see.

Teaching points
► You might include insects like those in idea 79, and printed lizards like those in idea 8.
► Ask the class to make things as 3-D as they can, pointing out various ways children have found to do this. Perhaps ask individual children to demonstrate to the class paper curling, twisting, etc.

Further activities
► Once you have created your rainforest it would be a pity not to use it as a starting point for writing individual or class poems.

45 Pond collages

Scope
Individual or group collages, using marbled papers as backgrounds

Age
9–11

Organisation
Individual or groups of 3 or 4

Time
1 hour (marbling to be done in advance)

Cross-curricular links
Science (pond life)

You will need
Copies of pcm 45 as needed; A4 or A3 marbled papers in shades of blue; variety of papers and thin card; glue and glue spreaders; wax crayons; newspaper to glue on; books on pond life

pcm 45 on page 85

Purpose
● To create a 3-D collage, using marbled papers as backgrounds.

Activity
1 Ask the children to print **marbled** paper in different shades of blue. This can be done in advance (*see* idea 25).
2 With the children, look at pictures of water lilies and other pond plants, pond animals and insects.
3 Demonstrate how to make a basic water lily (*see* pcm 45 for patterns).
4 Challenge the children to create dragonflies, frogs, newts, tadpoles and other pond creatures from paper and card. Frogs could be made from a folded piece of card so that they are symmetrical. Tell them to work out the pattern on scrap paper before cutting it in card.
5 If the children work in groups, they will need to join several sheets of paper together for the background.

6 Suggest that they make water lilies, insects and pond creatures, then put them on the background, trying out arrangements until they are happy with the composition.
7 Ask them to decide what else the picture needs: **collage** leaves, etc., or drawn tadpoles and weeds?

Teaching points
► Ponds can be rectangular, as the shape of the paper, or other irregular or symmetrical shapes.
► Older children may like to enlarge the collage to become an aerial view of a garden with paths, grass, flower beds, etc.

Further activities
► You might show the class a reproduction of Monet's 'Water Lilies' and discuss the work with them.
► Encourage the children to experiment with water lillies.

46 Silhouette collages

Scope
Individual collages using cut-out shapes on marbled paper backgrounds

Age
8–11

Organisation
Individual collages in whole class or groups

Time
1 hour (marbling to be done in advance)

Cross-curricular links
English (poems, stories, bible stories); could be used to illustrate a variety of topic work

You will need
marbled paper in any colours black paper; glue and glue spreaders; newspaper to glue on

pcm 46 on page 86

Purposes
● To use marbled papers in an imaginative way.
● To concentrate on the outline shape of things to produce a silhouette picture.

Activity
1 Ask the children to print marbled papers in advance, using a mixture of colours to achieve a wild effect (*see* idea 25).
2 If possible, show the children examples of silhouette pictures with interesting papers as backgrounds; for example, pictures in Jan Pienkowski's two books, *Easter* and *Christmas*. If you cannot find examples show the children examples of silhouettes in craft books on paper cuts.
3 Read the children 'The Witches Spell' from Macbeth (pcm 46). Show how the marbled papers could suggest wild and mysterious skies.
4 Ask the children to cut out shapes from the black paper to illustrate the poem and arrange them on the marbled backgrounds.

Teaching points
▶ As with all collage work, this activity gives the opportunity for arranging and rearranging a composition on a background if the pieces are not stuck down immediately.
▶ If the black pieces are fiddly to cut out and tear, they can be mended with glue and this will not show from a distance against the interesting marbled papers.

Further activities
▶ Marbled papers would make interesting backgrounds for city skyline pictures. The skylines (interesting rooftops, chimneys, etc.) could be cut out in several layers of shades of grey and black. This could be linked to drawing work on the local environment.

47 Under-sea collages

Scope
Collages in a variety of materials, using marbled papers as a background

Age
5–9

Organisation
Individual or groups

Time
1–1 1/2 hours (marbling to be done in advance)

Cross-curricular links
Science (sea life)

You will need
marbled papers in shades of blue and green (*see* idea 25); collage materials: variety of papers, polythene bags in any colours, wool, raffia, junk matrials such as polystyrene packaging shapes; glue and glue spreaders; newspaper to glue on; books showing life under the sea

Purposes
● To use marbled papers in an imaginative way.
● To handle a variety of materials and create **collages** with them.

Activity
1 With the children, look at pictures of life under the sea. Books will show that the variety of species is much richer than we can imagine! If you have a collection of shells and starfish, etc., show these too.
2 Talk about what materials might be used for under-sea collages; for instance, strips of polythene bag might be draped as seaweed, crumpled paper for rocks. Discuss how to make interesting fish of simple cut-out shapes. Say that any fish shapes are acceptable as there are so many different varieties in the sea. Discuss how you might represent a sea anenome, for example. Ask for suggestions.
3 Ask the children to make their own under sea collages on blue or green marbled papers (*see* idea 25), working either individually or in groups.

Teaching points
▶ With 5–6 year-olds you may need to provide cut-out fish shapes for the children to decorate with collage in various ways. Encourage them to make the fish as individual as they can, showing them pictures of the variety there is under the sea. Provide a selection for them to choose from, but allow any children capable of cutting their own to do so. You might prefer to do **bubble prints** as backgrounds for this age group.
▶ This activity could be done as a whole class collage if you joined the background papers together.
▶ You could add drawings of shells done from life to the collage.

Further activities
▶ With 9–11 year-olds, the collages could be done as 3-D scenes in cardboard boxes, with the marbled papers pasted on to the back to provide a background. This would take longer, but could be done in various scales and with different sized groups.

48 Mosaic pictures

Scope
Ideas for small mosaic pictures done to a theme that fit together to form a large piece of work

Age
8–11

Organisation
Groups of 2 or 3 per 'tile', working in whole class

Time
1 1/2 hours

Cross-curricular links
History (Romans), Science (harvest)

You will need
variety of coloured papers, including pages of colour magazines and supplements; glue and glue spreaders or glue sticks; squares of grey sugar paper approximately 25 cm square for 'tile' backgrounds; large sheets of paper; newspaper to glue on; books showing Roman mosaics

Purposes
● To investigate the making of mosaic pictures in Roman times.
● To reproduce the effects of Roman mosaics, using paper and other materials.

Activity
1 With the children, look at pictures of Roman mosaics, including an example with a border pattern, and talk about how these were made.
2 Choose a theme for the 'tiles' and get the children to do drawings of the chosen subject as preparation for making the mosaic pictures. Suitable themes, which need to be fairly simple, would include fruits and fish.
3 Demonstrate making a mosaic 'tile':
– Draw a simple shape on to the background paper.
– Cut small squares of coloured paper (about 1 cm square).
– Fill in the shape with these, sticking them down.
– Fill in the spaces round the picture with a chosen background colour.
4 Ask the children to make their own mosaic 'tiles' in groups of two or three.

Teaching points
► Point out that in real mosaics some of the background plaster shows around each mosaic piece, and this is partly what gives the mosaics their particular character.

► Ask the children to surround each 'tile' with a simple border of small pieces. This will set off the display when the tiles are assembled together.
► Finding interesting shades from colour supplements takes time but is worthwhile in terms of subtlety of the end result, especially for older children trying to reproduce real fruits and fish based on drawings from either books or life.
► A few groups could make a large border on a long thin strip of paper to surround the whole display. (Show them a reproduction of a Roman mosaic that has a border around it. One pattern was the scroll design.) Ask the children to draw some border designs and choose which would be most in keeping with the theme and which colours to do it in.

Further activities
► To make more chunky mosaic pieces, collect polystyrene food trays in as many colours as you can and make small pictures from these, stuck on sheets of card. They are easy to cut up into small squares and give the feel of real mosaic work more accurately; but the colour range is limited. You could try painting sheets with paint mixed with PVA glue before cutting them up.
► To depict a large figure in paper mosaic, draw it on to a background, then trace off different parts. Use the same colour background paper for each part. Give each part a different group to work on. Then cut round the finished parts and reassemble the figure before doing the background with more mosaic work. This way it is possible to do a large mosaic picture without it becoming too tedious for a single group. Supervise discussion on the colour scheme for the clothes. With top juniors you could try to reproduce a Roman design in this way.

49 Pasta and pulse collages

Scope
ictures and patterns made from dried pasta and pulses pressed into clay

Age
5–7

Organisation
Individual work in groups of 6

Time
1/2–3/4 hour

Cross-curricular links
Science (pulses)

You will need
nge of pasta shapes and dried pulses such as lentils, peas and beans in different colours; shallow plastic or polystyrene food trays; clay

Purpose
● To handle a variety of textured materials and make patterns with them.

Activity
1 Demonstrate how to press a lump of clay into the tray and smooth it down, to give a bed to press the pulses into, and how to press the pasta and pulses into the clay.
2 Talk about making a pattern with the pulses and pasta.

3 Ask the children to make their own pulses and pasta **collages**.

Teaching points
▶ Pulse and pasta can be stuck on to paper or card to make pictures but this is difficult for young children. If you decide to do this with older children use sheets of stiff card as pulses tend to fall off when pictures done on paper are moved.

50 Environmental collages

Scope
Pictures and patterns made from atural materials and photographed to record them

Age
5–11

Organisation
Individual or small groups (young children working with an adult)

Time
1 hour (longer if the children collect some of the materials themselves)

Cross-curricular links
Science (seasons, harvest)

You will need
range of leaves, seed pods, berries, twigs, petals, cereals, nuts and wild fruits, each type stored separately, as the palette (include leaves of various sizes, shapes and colours); lain surface to work on (this might be outdoors on a fine, still day); light coloured background cloth or paper if necessary; camera and colour film; books of environmental artists' work, such as Andy Goldsworthy, or *Approaches to Art* (Ginn)

Purpose
● To handle and sort a wide variety of natural materials.
● To experiment with making pictures and patterns with natural materials.

Activity
1 Show the children the work of an environmental artist such as Andy Goldsworthy's 'Maple Patch' which is in Ginn's art pack for primary schools, *Approaches to Art*. Talk about the possibilities this opens up.
2 Start off a simple pattern with a central motif and arrange some leaves around it. Ask the children to add something to the pattern, so that they get the idea. Show them that they can easily change their minds and remove pieces that don't seem to 'go'.
3 Ask the children to make their own environmental **collages**, either individually or in small groups.
4 Photograph the finished works. You could then have enlargements of the prints made on a colour photocopier and give the children photographs of their work.

Teaching points
▶ Autumn is an ideal time for this project.
▶ Pictures and patterns made in this way can be approached in a painterly fashion

by asking the children to consider the contrasts of colour, shape, size and tone in their work. Use tiny leaves and berries, etc., to add detail.
▶ Suitable subjects include birds, fish, people, geometric patterns, reptiles. Ask the children to think what any unusual leaves suggest to them.
▶ It is easier to photograph the works if they are done on the floor or ground.
▶ This is a messy project but the results and experience are worth the mess!

Further activities
▶ Pictures on a smaller scale, using leaves, conifer twigs, seeds, etc., stuck on to white paper, can be photocopied. The materials need to be flattish to do this, so you won't be able to use berries. Cut small circles of black paper instead. Try for yourself the effects of photocopying leaves, ash tree keys, etc., and show the children how these print. Try birds, fish, hedgehogs, reptiles, faces. This process of experiment is best done with older children (10–11 year-olds).
▶ For young children you may like to consider having a box of stones, shells, twigs and feathers in the classroom as a resource with which to make non-permanent pictures and patterns which are displayed for a day or so before being dismantled.

Painting

See pcm on page 78 for examples of painting and pastel techniques

Basic equipment

Depending on activity select from:

- paints, powder or readymix – white, lemon yellow, scarlet, crimson, blue, turquoise, black
- mixing palettes
- paintbrushes, large and fine
- water jars
- chalks
- pencils
- white cartridge paper
- grey sugar paper
- masking tape

If you feel unsure of your own artistic abilities, there are still lots of useful painting activities and opportunities you can offer the children, and many simple techniques that you can practise yourself beforehand, then demonstrate to the class. Some of these are:

Colour-mixing

I suggest starting each painting session with a brief demonstration of mixing colours, as a reminder to the children. To avoid wasting paint, teach the children to mix secondary colours using the lightest primary colour first, then adding the second, darker one, a little at a time, until the desired shade is achieved. Thus, to mix green, start with yellow, then add blue, only a little at a time because it's such a strong colour. Similarly, to mix orange, start with yellow, then add scarlet, a little at a time; to mix purple, start with crimson and add royal blue. To mix brown, mix orange, then add royal blue, a little at a time. If you add too much blue and the paint goes greenish, you will need to add a bit more scarlet. To make a dark brown, you will need to add black, a tiny bit at a time.

When teaching the mixing of light tones, teach the children always to start with the white paint, then add the other colour, a little at a time.

Five- to seven-year-olds paint pictures in a very immediate and emotionally involved way. For many, the insistence on mixing colours on a palette would be an intrusion. But there is another approach you might like to try where colour mixing occurs on the paper. For this you need white paper, the three primary colours in dry powder paint, a brush and a jar of water. Teach the children the simple routine of washing the brush, then dipping it into the dry paint before applying the brush to the paper. This routine is simple to remember and non-intrusive, the effect akin to watercolour painting.

Colour-mixing is best taught in a fairly structured way. For eight- to eleven-year olds, ideally only white, lemon yellow, royal blue, scarlet, crimson and black should be available. From these it is possible to mix a very wide range of colours and tones. You need two shades of red to mix good shades of orange and purple. If you sometimes need a greater range of greens, you could add turquoise to the colours above.

Brush techniques

Challenge the children at the start of a painting session to discover for themselves how many ways they can apply the paint and how many effects the can achieve. Paint can be used really thickly and dabbed on, colours allowed to mix on the paper, applied in broad sweeping strokes, flicked on, etc. Look at the experiments and discuss them, stick some of them up and label them (see pcm on page 78). Remind the children of these experiments at the next session.

'Water colour' technique

Try using very watery paint on white cartridge pap (see idea 56).

Starting a painting

Show the children how to draw freely with a brush and very pale grey wash before using colour when they are painting. Insist that they start a painting this way, or use chalks to draw the shapes freely, not pencil. Emphasise that painting is not just a drawing coloured in or painted over.

Mixed media work

Encourage a wide approach to painting. Painting, properly taught, is a problem-solving activity – anything is acceptable as long as it gives the effect that you want. The children could try paint on textured paper collage, chalk or pastels over paint, wax crayons over paint, etc.

Pastel work

This is generally regarded as a painting technique. Many of the subjects listed below would be suitabl for pastel work.

Starting points for painting

- The children's own experiences (most appropriate for five- to seven-year olds).

- Stories (also appropriate for younger children) – use discussion first to enrich the children's ideas. With older children you could use passages from longer books as starting points.

- Poems – can be descriptive or 'atmospheric'.

- Prints of works of art – focus on a particular aspect such as matching the colours, or a technique such as using thick **impasto** paint (mix polyfilla powder or washing powder into the paint) or use them for inspiration.

- Sketching – nine- to eleven-year olds might sketch trees, buildings, etc., as a basis for painting.

51 Painted leaves

Scope
Colour-mixing exercise (four shades of orange) using leaf shapes as a focus

Age
7–8
(9–11 year-olds could do a more complex version of the activity)

Organisation
Individual work in whole class

Time
3/4–1 hour

Cross-curricular links
Science (autumn)

You will need
leaves as templates;
white paper;
yellow and scarlet paints;
paintbrushes; water jars;
mixing palette for each child

Purpose

● To mix shades of one colour from primary colours.

Activity

1 Demonstrate drawing leaves and mixing **shades** of orange to paint them:

– Draw round four leaves on the paper.

– On the palette, mix a light orange, starting with yellow and adding a very little red.

– Paint one of the leaves with this.

– Now show how, by adding a little more red to the orange, a deeper orange can be mixed.

– Paint another leaf with this.

2 Ask the children to draw and paint their own four leaves in shades of orange.

Teaching points

► Train the children to start with the lightest colour first, starting with yellow and adding the red a little at a time. If you decide to do greens, the process is similar: start with the yellow and add blue. Tell the children that they are mixing *four shades of one colour*.

► Do not allow the children to use white to lighten the colours. If you use white you are mixing light **tones** which is a separate colour-mixing exercise.

► When they are dry, the leaves can be cut out and used for a class project to make an autumn tree, or arranged as a large pattern.

► Older children might be asked to mix six or eight shades of orange or green.

Further activities

► A further use of leaves in different shades would be to use the shapes to create a frame round the edge of a large sheet of paper and ask the children to paint an autumn scene inside it. This would combine colour-mixing, imaginative work and observation.

► Suggest ideas for the scenes inside the leaf frames by reading poems or by discussion. When the paint is dry, pastels can be used over the paint, if liked; this would be a good way to put in detail of the veins on the leaves.

52 Stained glass windows

Scope
Collages of strips of black paper, used as patterns for colour-mixing exercises

Age
9–11

Organisation
Collage 'windows': individual work in whole class;
painting: individual work in groups or whole class, depending on facilities

Time
Collage windows: 1/2 hour;
painting: 1 hour (could be 2 sessions)

You will need
A3 white paper;
black sugar paper;
glue and glue spreaders;
two primary colours (select from yellow and blue, yellow and red, crimson and royal blue);
paintbrushes;
water jars;
mixing palette for each child

Purposes
● To practise tearing skills.
● To make a pleasing pattern with the torn paper strips.
● To mix and use **shades** of secondary colours from primary colours.

Activity
1 Demonstrate making a grid from torn strips of black paper:
– Remind children that paper has a 'grain' and tears more easily into strips in one direction than another.
– Tear several strips and then arrange these on a sheet of white paper until you like the pattern they make.
– Stick them down.
– Use any small pieces to make the shapes or edges more interesting. (You need to form about ten or twelve spaces.)
– Explain that the **collages** will have the appearance of a stained glass window when the shapes have been painted in.
2 Ask the children to make their own collage 'windows'.
3 Then demonstrate colour-mixing, using one of the two-colour combinations listed under 'You will need'. (*See* Introduction to painting, page 38 and idea 51 for details of colour-mixing.)
4 Ask the children to mix shades of their two colours to fill in their 'windows'.

Teaching points
▶ Encourage the children to mix as many different shades of their chosen colours as they can, and to try to fill in each section of the window with a different shade, if possible.
▶ You may like to give older children a little of the third primary colour as well, so that they can, for example, mix a slightly browny purple by adding a little yellow to the red and blue.
▶ When looking at the finished work, there are two main things to focus on: the shapes of the grids and how pleasing these are and the range of colours mixed.
▶ Allow discussion of the colours and perhaps name some of them.
▶ Mount the finished works on black paper for a dramatic effect or arrange them all close together to make a large window.

Further activities
▶ Collect some very large leaves, and draw round one. Draw in some of the veins to make about ten or twelve sections. Go over the lines with wax crayons, and fill each section of the leaf with a different shade of green or orange.

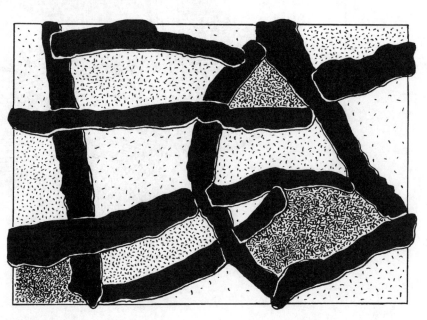

53 Colour-mixing tones

Scope
Structured exercise in mixing tones of one colour

Age
8–11

Organisation
Individual work in whole class

Time
1/2 hour

You will need
A3 white cartridge paper; white and one chosen primary colour; paintbrushes; water jars; mixing palette for each child

Purpose
● To teach the mixing of **tones** of a colour in a structured way.

Activity
1 Demonstrate the colour-mixing exercise:
– Lay the paper down landscapewise.
– Draw five interesting wiggly lines across the paper at various intervals. (Variation in distances between the lines will add to the interest.) Fill in the top section of the paper with white paint.
– Put some white paint on the mixing palette and add a very small amount of your chosen primary colour to it, to make a very pale colour.
– Use this in the section next to the one painted white.
– Now add another small amount of your chosen colour to the very pale colour on your mixing palette, to make a slightly deeper tone.
– Use this in the next section down on the painting.
– Continue in this way until you have filled all the sections, finishing with the primary colour on its own.
2 Ask the children to do their own painting in sections.

Teaching points
▶ Older children might be challenged to make more than five tones of their chosen colour.
▶ Tell the children that they are mixing *tones of one colour* and that they can make darker tones by adding black to a chosen colour, too.

Further activities
▶ When the paintings are dry, they could be used as background skies (in any colour) for a cut-out skyline silhouette in black paper. Or they might be used for collage work: vases could be cut out of them for flower collages, or stripy fish for an under-sea work.
▶ This colour-mixing exercise could be used to create a patchwork flower from seven hexagon shapes, filling each shape with a different tone of the chosen colour. These flower shapes could be cut out when dry and joined together to make a class patchwork quilt. (Show the children some illustrations of patchwork quilts.)
▶ Any of the above exercises would be useful as introductory sessions before doing idea 54.

54 Painting in tones of blue

Scope
Painting, using the skills practised in the formal colour-mixing exercise in idea 53

Age
8–11

Organisation
Individual work in whole class or groups according to space and facilities

Time
1 hour

Cross-curricular links
Science (seasons), English (stories, poems)

You will need
white or grey paper; blue or white chalk; blue and white paint; paintbrushes; water jars; mixing palette for each child

Purpose
● To give the opportunity to use the skills of colour-mixing learned in idea 53 in an imaginative composition.

Activity
1 Discuss Jack Frost, a fabulous blue bird which should be painted in **tones** of blue, or a blue planet where everything, including the inhabitants, are blue.
2 Demonstrate drawing on the paper in chalk, blue if using white paper, white if using grey paper. Remind the children that when painting they do not need to make a very detailed drawing as they will be painting over it. Emphasise that painting is not just a drawing coloured in.

3 Then demonstrate mixing tones of blue, especially if the colour-mixing exercise in idea 53 was done some time previously .
4 Ask the children to do their own painting in tones of blue, illustrating the theme you discussed.

Teaching points
▶ You may decide to allow small amounts of other colours when the paintings are nearing completion. If you choose the coloured planet theme, perhaps one group could paint in tones of blue, another in tones of red and another in tones of yellow. Aliens painted in these tones would be fun to do, as would aliens' dinners in the same tones.

55 Paintings in shades of green

Scope
Painting, using skills practised in the formal colouring exercise in idea 53

Age
8–11

Organisation
Individual work in whole class groups, depending on space and facilities

Time
1–1 1/2 hours

Cross-curricular links
English (myths and legends)

You will need
white or grey paper; yellow, green or white chalk; paint in yellow, royal blue and a little red; paintbrushes; water jars; mixing palette for each child; leaves or pictures of dragons

Purpose
● To give the opportunity to use the skills of colour-mixing learned in idea 53 in an imaginative painting.

Activity
1 Discuss the legend of the Green Man, a mythical figure written about in the Middle Ages who lived in woods and forests and whose face was made of leaves; or the story of St George and the Dragon.
2 Demonstrate drawing on the paper in chalk (*see* idea 54). Use yellow or green chalk with white paper, white with grey paper.
3 Then demonstrate mixing shades of green to illustrate the chosen legend, always starting with the lightest colour first, in this case the yellow (so avoiding much waste paint) and adding blue. And show how mixing a tiny amount of red into green gives a brownish green.
4 Ask the children to do their own paintings of the chosen legend.

Teaching points
► You may decide to allow small amount of other colours to be used when the paintings are nearly finished. Discuss with the children what colour background would 'set off' the leafy faces of the Green Man to best advantage, or suggest that the faces be almost disguised in a leafy background.

56 Water colour skies

Scope
Experimenting with paints on wet paper

Age
8–11

Organisation
Individual work in groups, size depending on space and facilities

Time
3/4 hour

You will need
good quality A3 white cartridge paper; masking tape; drawing boards if available; clean sponges (optional); small amounts of paint in royal blue, yellow, scarlet and crimson; large paintbrushes; water jars; mixing palette for each child

Purpose
● To experiment with the effects that can be obtained using washes of paint on wet paper.

Activity
1 Demonstrate painting on wet paper to produced the effect of coloured skies:
– Tape the paper to a board or a Formica table top with masking tape all around the edge. (If you do not have space for this or boards to use, you can still try these techniques, but the papers will not dry very flat.)
– Dampen the paper all over with water, using a large paintbrush or clean sponge.
– Mix some paint to a watery wash, the consistency of ink.
– Apply some of this to the paper.
– Mix a second colour and paint some on to the paper. (Where the colours meet they will flood into each other.)
– Mix a third coloured wash and add this to the paper. (You might also try dropping some of this on to the first two colours.)

2 Ask the children to make their own paintings on wet paper.

Teaching points
► If you use readymix paint, the colours will be soft and subtle. If you would like bolder effects, for a sky at sunset for instance, try working with coloured inks Bear in mind, however, that inks stain.
► Leave the wet papers to dry on the boards or tables. When they are dry, carefully peel the masking tape off. Papers taped to the table tops at the end of school will have all night to dry.
► Masking tape is cheap to buy from decorating shops and leaves no sticky marks.

Further activities
► Use these papers as backgrounds for either **collage** work or silhouette scenes in black ink. Suggest that the children base the silhouette scenes on observational drawings of rooftops or winter trees, for example.

57 Pastel work techniques

Scope
Ideas for teaching a variety of pastel work techniques

Age
8–11

Organisation
Individual work in whole class

Time
Experiments: 1/2 hour; picture: 3/4 hour

You will need
pastels and coloured chalks; sugar paper in a variety of deep shades, including black, large and small sheets

Purpose
● To teach a variety of techniques suitable for a specific medium.

Activity
1 Challenge the children to suggest as many ways of using the pastel as they can think of.
2 Try the strokes they suggest as they watch.
3 Add your own suggestions from your own experience or the list in 'Teaching points' and demonstrate these too. (Ask, *What would be a good way of getting the effect of fur?* for example.)
4 Ask the children to try out all these ways on a small piece of sugar paper.
5 Ask them to make a picture using, say, at least three of the techniques to add interest to the work. (It's up to you how many you stipulate.)
6 Encourage them to keep their sheet of 'try outs' and to use this as they work out specific effects.

Teaching points
► Remind the children of the techniques to try, if they have not already suggested them: using the pastels on their side, so that the grain of paper is revealed; making a series of strokes side by side; blocking in areas fairly solidly; blending colours together; smudging areas to give a soft blurred effect; making a series of small dots or dashes, either in one colour or several (*see* pcm on page 78 for some examples).

► Do not allow the children to draw in pencil first. The whole work should be executed in chalks or pastels. Oil pastels are a separate medium and require different handling.

► Ideas for subject matter for pastel work: space pictures; our favourite soft toys (try to get the fur effects); animal pictures done from borrowed museum specimens or photographs; still lifes of flowers or fruits, done from life.

Further activities
► Look at some works in pastels by famous artists, for instance Degas, Toulouse-Lautrec, the dream-like flower studies of the French artist Odilon Redon. Can the children identify some of the techniques used and compare them with their own experiments?

58 Pastel word pictures

Scope
Imaginative pictures drawn round a word

Age
8–11

Organisation
Individual work in whole class

Time
1 hour

Cross-curricular links
Science (seasons, seasonal events)

You will need
chalk type pastels; sugar paper in a variety of deep shades; scrap paper

Purpose
● To use the pastel techniques practised in idea 57 in an imaginative way.

Activity
1 Draw the word 'WINTER' boldly across the paper in chunky lettering.
2 Talk about how this might become part of a winter scene, for example by drawing snow on the tops of the letters; or arranging the letters on a slope and devise a sledging scene around them; or forming the letters from a wall or bare winter twigs.
3 Encourage the children to suggest their own ideas. Ask, *What does winter make you think of?*
4 Ask the children to make their own pastel picture round the word 'winter', or some other word.

Teaching points
► Remind the children to try out the pastel techniques discussed in project 57 before they start work. Give them small pieces of scrap paper for this. Ask them to think about which technique best suggests the texture that they want.

► Tell the children to draw the word *faintly* until they are sure it is as they want it to be. Pastels will rub out to some extent but this is to be avoided if possible as it spoils the surface of the sugar paper quite quickly.

Further activities
► 9–11 year-olds might be asked to find examples of lettering they like in newspapers and magazines, and to try to copy the style.

► This activity works well for incorporating adjectives into a picture, using words like 'twiggy', 'leafy', 'snowy', and words such as 'bonfire' and 'patterned'. Challenge the children to think of other words that they might illustrate this way.

Drawing

See pcm on page 79
for examples of
drawing techniques

Basic equipment

Five to seven years

- pencils, HB and 2B
- chalks, white and coloured
- wax crayons, thick and thin
- felt pens
- colouring pencils
- oil pastels
- range of coloured sugar papers
- smooth white paper

Eight to eleven years

As above with addition of:

- charcoal and charcoal pencils
- pastels
- water-soluble colouring pencils
- biros
- pen or sharpened sticks and ink (nine to eleven years)
- good quality cartridge paper paper for special projects

Detailed below is a brief description of the stages that children go through in their artistic development at primary level. These developmental stages relate to the drawing activities it is appropriate to offer them, and these, too, are indicated below. The ages at which the children go through the stages vary widely, *but it is important to remember that each child goes through all the stages and that he or she needs to do so*, moving from one stage to another in a continuous way.

The scribbling stage (two to four years, though many five- and some six-year-olds are still at this stage)

- An important 'play' stage of discovery.
- Children move gradually from random mark-making to beginning to control the marks they make.
- Development of earliest representations of human face and figure. These early drawing experiences are important for development of hand/eye co-ordination and fine motor skills.
- Children draw their experiences, not what they see.

The pre-schematic stage (approximately four to seven years)

- Children gradually develop personal 'schema' or symbols for things they want to draw often: mummy, tree, house, etc.
- Children very emotionally involved in their work.
- Six- and seven-year-olds can sometimes be asked to observe and record simple objects.
- Drawing of experience and as self-expression should predominate.
- A range of drawing materials should be offered.

The schematic stage (approximately seven to nine years)

- Children refine their symbols and add greater detail to their drawings.
- Refining process can be encouraged – ask

children to observe and sketch details of real houses, people, animals, flowers, trees, etc.

- Children can be asked to look at outside world and record from observation – details such as patterns of brickwork, patterns on butterfly's wings veins on leaf, ironwork grille, etc.
- Children should be offered *choice* of drawing materials and encouraged to choose appropriate medium for subject matter as they mature.
- Begin to teach simple drawing techniques, such as different ways of using pencils.

The dawning of realism stage (ten to thirteen years)

- Children become more aware of the world around them, want to be able to draw realistically.
- Dissatisfaction with work and loss of confidence if they don't have skills to do so.
- Need for activities to overcome loss of confidence and consequent lack of interest: specific techniques such as shading with hatching and cross-hatching (*see* idea 60), drawing lightly until everything in right place and proportion, using faint lines down centre of symmetrical object (*see* ideas 61 and 62).
- Need for more activities with opportunities to draw from observation, with help (*see* ideas 60–62).
- Drawing unfamiliar objects helps overcome problem of being over self-critical (children less ready to judge work as 'looking wrong') – minute objects seen through magnifying glass, for instance (bird's leg, crab's claw, half peeled apple or satsuma, etc.). Suggest using scrap paper to try out ways of representing texture, for example.
- Children should often be offered a choice of media. This is fairly simple to arrange with drawing activities. When looking at finished work with the children, compare the different effects obtained and which medium seems most suited to a particular topic.

59 Imaginary lands

Scope
Drawings done from a 'starter' line given to each child

Age
6–9

Organisation
Individual work in whole class

Time
3/4–1 hour

Cross-curricular links
English (imaginative writing and story-telling)

You will need
A3 white paper; pencils; coloured pencils (optional)

Purpose
● To stimulate the children's imaginative drawing.

Activity
1   In advance, draw an interesting and varied line across each sheet of paper, roughly in the middle, to represent the outline of a section of land or possibly coast and sea. Have the paper landscape way round.
2   Show the children one of the prepared sheets of paper and talk about the fact that the line represents a section of land. Any land. Suggest that the peaks could be mountains, and that the troughs might

be valleys or even seas. It can be any type of land they like. Talk about the possibility of showing what is under the ground as well. The drawings can include trees, buildings, people, vehicles, machines. Ask, *What might people be doing on mountains? What might be under the ground?* (miners, caves, animals, fossils, etc.)
3   Ask the children to develop their own land drawings around the lines on their paper.

Teaching points
▶ Encourage the children to put lots of detail into these pictures. What could be happening in the sky, for example?

Further activities
▶ You might suggest that the line represents the surface of another planet. Try to give a slightly different line for this, maybe curving it slightly to suggest a convex shape, but still making it a varied and interesting line.

60 The old boots

Scope
Ideas for observational drawing sessions

Age
9–11

Organisation
Individual work; group size to enable active teacher involvement with children drawing

Time
1–1 1/2 hours

You will need
white cartridge paper; drawing boards, if available; masking tape; 2B and HB pencils; pair of boots or shoes; copies of pcm 60 as needed; book of Van Gogh's work

pcm 60 on page 87

Purpose
● To study and represent realistically a given subject.

Activity
1   With the children, look at Van Gogh's picture of an old pair of boots, to be found in most comprehensive works on Van Gogh. Talk about the detail in the work, and invite the children to say anything that they notice about it.
2   Arrange the boots or shoes to be drawn in front of the group of children. Raise them up slightly on an upturned box if necessary, so that everyone in the group has a good view.
3   Show the children how to rest their drawing boards at an angle against the edge of the table, the lower edges on their laps. This gives a good position for drawing.

4   Show them how to fix sheets of paper to the boards with masking tape.
5   Remind them to draw lightly until they are sure that they have things in the right proportion and position. Tell them that you want a detailed study of the boots, but to get the drawing done in broad outline before they put the details in.
6 Ask the children to draw the boots.

Teaching points
▶ Go round each of the children in turn and discuss their work with them. Praise any work that is well-observed, even if it is not particularly accurate in other ways, because this exercise is particularly about close observation.

▶ When the drawings are well under way, suggest that the children vary the pressure they apply to their pencils, thereby varying the lines they make.

▶ Remind 9–11 year-olds about how to do shading. (You may like to ask them to do the exercise on cross-hatching on pcm 60 for practise before they tackle the boots.)

▶ Look at the drawings with the children when they have finished, and ask questions to focus their attention on any particular aspects of the work you have asked them to consider.

Further activities

▶ Other simple drawing projects suitable for this age group include drawing hands in an interesting position or holding something (show Dürer's famous engraving of praying hands), feet, twigs and small natural objects such as shells, a crab's claw, seed pods, etc. (using a magnifying lens).

  # 61 Drawing a portrait

Scope
Guidelines on drawing a portrait

Age
9–11

Organisation
Individual work in whole or half class

Time
1/2–3/4 hour

Cross-curricular links
History (historical portraits such as Tudor miniatures)

You will need
copies of pcm 61 for each child (mask off half the picture with folded A4 paper when photocopying; give copies of the left-hand side to right-handed children and vice versa); pencils and rubbers

pcm 61 on page 88

Purpose
● To teach children to look at proportions of the face and features when drawing a portrait.

Activity
1 Give out pcm 61 and tell the children that they will be finishing off the face.
2 Before they start, look with them at some of the important points to bear in mind when drawing a portrait (demonstrate on the board if you are confident about drawing, or point them out with a child posing for you):
– The eyes come about two-fifths of the way down the head. (Children often draw them very high up.)
– Eyebrows are not just a line, but made up of lots of hairs, all pointing in a particular direction. The children should use short pencil strokes to achieve this look.
– The eyelids have a dark line of deep shadow over them.
– The lips have a dark line of deep shadow separating them.
– The nostrils appear dark because they, too, are dark shadow.
– There is approximately the width of an eye between the eyes.

– Eyeballs are circular but the eyelid cuts off the circle a bit.
– Eyelashes are fine and delicate, so should be drawn lightly in pencil.
3 Ask the children to complete the copymaster portraits.

Further activities

▶ After practising the points above, using the pcm, children could be asked to draw a portrait of themselves or a classmate in pencil. Ask them to observe the shadows and try to shade in areas of the face to 'model' the portrait. (Get the children to practise shading first. Remind them of the main points that they have observed in the copymaster portrait.)

▶ Talk to the children about how people always used to be portrayed in their best clothes, and suggest that they draw themselves or their classmate in their best clothes or a special outfit.

▶ Mention that the artist often provides clues about the sitter's interests or hobbies in a portrait. This could provide another starting point for a portrait.

▶ The children could try doing the miniatures in coloured pencils. (Get them to do some hatching and cross-hatching exercises first, *see* pcm 60.)

62 Drawing a simple still life

Scope
Drawing exercise to teach children to draw ellipses

Age
9–11

Organisation
Individual work in whole class

Time
Copymaster exercise: 1/2 hour; follow-up drawing session: 3/4 hour

You will need
variety of cups and jars – can be plastic; pcm 62 for each child (mask off half the picture with folded A4 paper when photocopying; give copies of the left-hand side to right-handed children and vice versa); pencils and rubbers

pcm 62 on page 89

Purpose
● To teach the children to look at the ellipse shapes at the top of cups, jars, etc., and to draw them.

Activity
1 Look at the real cups and jars.
2 Give each child a cup and ask them to hold them down on their laps, so that the top appears as a circle.
3 Ask them to lift up the cups gradually so the circle appears as an ellipse. Point out to them that it is still a circle, but that it appears to be a different shape.
4 Now tell them to put the cups on top of their desks and point out that the bottoms of the cups appear as curved lines, where they sit on the desks.
5 Give out pcm 62 and ask the children first to try drawing some ellipse shapes freely with a flowing line, then to try to complete the drawings, making the objects as symmetrical as they can. The dotted line down the centre of the objects should help with this.

Teaching points
► Look at the drawings with the class, and praise the children's efforts.
► You may like to suggest that they draw the plastic cups after completing the pcms. Remind them that they can draw a faint line down the centre of the cup to help them draw both sides symmetrically.
► Encourage them to complete their drawings with areas of shading.

Further activities
► Set up simple arrangements of cups, bowls, etc., for the children to draw. Encourage them to look at the shapes between the objects as well as the actual objects. I use some bottles and jars painted with white emulsion paint as simple objects to draw. (Painting the bottles white simplifies them as there are no distracting reflections.)
► With the class, look at some paintings of still lifes from various periods.

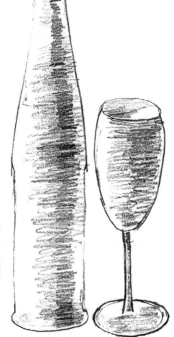

63 Cross-stitch 'samplers'

Scope
Designs based on observation of Victorian cross-stitch work

Age
7–11

Organisation
Individual work in whole class, best done in 2 sessions

Time
First experiments and discussion: 1 hour; final designs: 2 hours

Cross-curricular links
History (Victorians)

You will need
sheets of 5 mm squared paper for each child (A4 and A3 – for A3 copy twice and run off A3 sheets from this if necessary); fine felt-tipped pens or colouring pencils; books on embroidery or the Victorians showing samplers

Purpose

● To design a sampler using a squared format.

● To look at reproductions of Victorian samplers.

● To build up letter shapes and designs using a single simple 'stitch'.

Activity

1 With the children, look at examples of Victorian samplers. (These can be found in books on embroidery and on the Victorians. You may also be able to borrow real examples from your local museum loans service.) Talk about the samplers and the fact that these were often done by young children.

2 Demonstrate on A4 squared paper how to build up a pattern and letters by putting a cross in each square to represent a stitch.

3 Suggest to the children that they try out their designs and some patterns for borders, on their A4 'rough' sheets. Talk

about simple design ideas that it would be possible to achieve with this technique: houses, trees, plants (in pots), animals, faces, etc.

4 Assemble the experimental A4 sheets and discuss them. Ask the children to say what they think was successful and what didn't work so well before moving on to the A3 squared paper and their full designs.

Teaching points

► Point out to the children that they will need to count the squares if they want to centre their designs.

► Provide another sheet of A4 squared paper for them to try out further ideas.

Further activities

► Older children might like to embroider their designs on linen or squared embroidery fabric.

► You might also refer to samplers from other eras, such as the Tudor period, and other cultures.

64 Wax-resist patterns

Scope
Introduction to wax resist technique

Age
7–11

Organisation
Wax patterns: whole class; inking: group of about 6 at separate table

Time
1 1/2 hours

You will need
white paper, A3 or A4; wax crayons, thick and thin; powdered inks in about 6 colours, made up with water (if not available, school paints watered down to wash); separate paintbrush in each jar; newspaper to cover table; aprons

Purpose

● To introduce the children to **wax-resist** technique in a structured way.

Activity

1 Arrange a separate table for the inking. Inks stain, so cover the table with newspaper and provide the children with aprons.

2 Demonstrate making a wax-resist pattern:

– Draw faint pencil lines across a sheet of paper at irregular intervals.

– On these draw patterns of loops, circles, etc., based on letter shapes.

– Go over the pencil lines with wax crayon, pressing hard so a heavy deposit of wax is left on the paper which will resist the inks.

– Paint over your pattern with various coloured inks. The coloured inks should remain separated by the wax lines, and

the patterns will show up more clearly against the inked background

3 Ask the children to make their own wax-resist patterns.

Teaching points

► Any school paints watered down to a wash may be used instead of inks but the colour contrasts will not be so sharp and pleasing.

► Check that the lines and patterns have been drawn clearly enough to resist the ink.

► Tell the children to brush over the patterns with the inks or paints quite quickly. If they 'scrub' at an area, the wax may not resist the ink well.

► Discuss which ink colours set off the coloured wax lines most effectively. With older children, you might discuss complementary colours in connection with this.

Further activities

► Younger children could draw fish shapes and fill these outlines with rows of patterns.

► Follow up this introductory activity with another wax-resist project to build on the skills acquired (*see* ideas 65 and 66). Let the children keep these experimental sheets as references for their next project.

► Read the class 'The Centipede's Song' from *James and the Giant Peach* by Roald Dahl. Ask the children to draw jar shapes and to fill these with insects, etc., to make items suitable for a centipede's or witch's pantry.

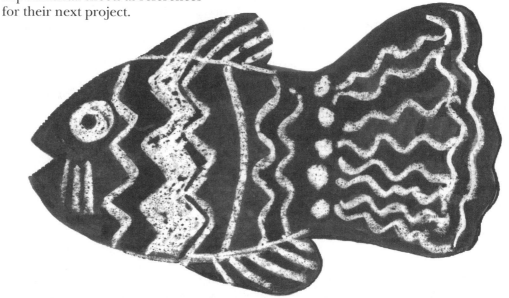

65 Vase of flowers

Scope
Further activity for using wax-resist techniques

Age
7–11

Organisation
Wax drawings: whole class or groups; inking: group of about 6 at separate table

Time
1 1/2 hours

You will need
vase of flowers or prints of flower paintings;
A3 white paper ;
wax crayons, thick and thin;
black and dark blue ink or watery paint;
wide paintbrushes;
newspapers to cover table; aprons

Purpose
● To explore further the technique of **wax-resist**.

Activity
1 With the children, look at the vase of flowers or flower paintings.

2 Demonstrate drawing a flower in wax crayon, then washing over it with black or dark blue ink so that the wax resists the ink (*see* idea 64).

3 Ask the children to do their own wax-resist flower paintings.

Teaching points
► Inks are best for this activity as they have a good covering capacity and will make the colours of the wax glow.

► Remind the children to press quite hard so that a good deposit of wax is laid on to the surface of the paper. When they come to paint over their work, remind

them not to scrub with the paint or ink. Young children especially tend to scrub the paper.

► These pictures look most effective when painted all over with the dark ink, but if you want to supply other colours, that's up to you.

Further activities
► Younger children might like to try drawing a picture of a bonfire or fireworks, then brushing it over with black ink. Or they could try Christmas tree pictures, using white wax for some of the lights and see how this shows up when painted over with black or dark blue.

► You may like to extend this project to include observational drawing of the vase of flowers for the children to draw first. Do the wax drawings as a separate session after this.

66 Patchwork quilt patterns

Scope
Wax-resist pictures of toys in bed, with patchwork quilts

Age
7–9

Organisation
Wax patterns: whole class; inking: group of 6 at separate table

Time
1 1/2 hours

You will need
A3 white paper ; scrap paper; wax crayons, thick and thin; inks or paints as described in idea 64; wide paintbrushes; newspapers to cover table; aprons samples of patterned fabrics or books of quilts (optional)

Purposes
● To practice **wax-resist** technique.
● To develop pattern-making skills and ideas.

Activity
1 Arrange a separate table for the inking (*see* idea 64).
2 Show the children samples of patterned fabrics or examples of quilts in books.
3 Demonstrate making a wax-resist picture of a toy in bed:
– Working with the paper portrait way round, lightly draw a line across the paper approximately one third of the way down. The top section will form the pillow of the bed, the section below will become the patterned quilt.
– In the bottom section, draw two lines across the paper and two lines down the paper to form nine rectangles.
– Working in wax crayon, draw a different pattern in each of the small rectangles. Go over the pencil lines with wax lines.
– Draw a teddy or other toy in the bed with just the face showing on the pillow area.

– Demonstrate going over each section of the picture with different coloured inks.
4 Ask the children to make their own wax-resist pictures.

Teaching points
▶ Discuss and ask for suggestions about the types of patterns to be found in dress fabrics.
▶ Discuss how the children might achieve the effect of a teddy bear's fur, for instance, and allow them to try out some effects on scrap paper.
▶ Remind them to press hard with the wax crayons and to brush over the wax fairly quickly with the inks.

Further activities
▶ Older children might prefer to draw themselves or a character from a book in bed, or just do the whole sheet as a patchwork quilt. As in the main activity, you might like to bring in some patterned fabrics or examples of quilts in books, to look at.

Model-making and papier-mâché work

See pcm on page 80 for examples of model making and papier-mâché work

Most of the ideas for model-making and papier-mâché work in this section offer a structured approach, in which a basic structure and various techniques are demonstrated to the children. Within this lies a great deal of flexibility: children can adapt the basic idea, and indeed should be encouraged to do so, as a vehicle for their own ideas so that, hopefully, each child's model will be highly individual when finished.

As with all projects in the primary school, a balance needs to be struck between the teaching and learning of practical skills necessary for the activity, and self-expression. The above approach offers an opportunity to fulfil both these aspects, and is also a practical way of working for the busy classroom teacher.

With five- to seven-year-olds, as well as the structured activities suggested, there should be sessions on making models from junk materials, with the children either looking at junk items and seeing what they suggest, or having an idea that they want to carry out, such as making a vehicle, and trying to make it from what's available. Both approaches are equally valid and represent two different creative approaches.

Model-making is a messy activity but mess can be kept to a minimum by establishing good working routines.

Teaching children to make artifacts and work confidently with their hands should lead to life-long skills and confidence in their ability to make things.

Practical tips for model-making and papier-mâché work:

● Teach children to tear newspaper. Show that newspaper tears easily into strips in one direction, not in the other.

● Masking tape is better than Sellotape for model-making as it is made of paper and can be painted and pasted over easily.

● When strengthening a model with layers of newspaper and paste, provide coloured newspaper for alternate layers, enabling the children to keep a count of the layers.

● In papier-mâché work, teach the children to overlap the strips of paper and to smooth them down well as they work.

● The children can use brushes or fingers to paste the papers.

● If they use too much paste and the model starts to get very soggy, tell them to apply a layer of dry paper and smooth this down to soak up the excess paste.

● To achieve a good result with school paints on papier-mâché work, it's a good idea to finish with a layer of plain newsprint or paint a base coat over the dry model first. White, quick drying acrylic undercoat is useful for this. Emulsion tends to resist school paints.

Basic equipment

Depending on the activity, select from:

● junk materials - bottles, jars, plastic bottles and containers, yogurt pots, packaging, buttons, sequins, tinsel, wool, raffia, feathers, dried pasta, pipe cleaners, etc.

● fabrics including felt, lace, etc.

● papers - tissue, coloured, colour supplements, foil, cellophane, doilies, etc.

● newspapers, including coloured and plain newsprint

● card
● cardboard boxes including shoe boxes
● cardboard tubes
● sticks such as garden prunings
● art straws
● Plasticine
● brass fasteners

● plaster bandage
● rolls of cotton wool
● scissors
● needles and thread
● pins
● staplers
● Vaseline or cling film
● PVA glue

● cellulose paste
● thick paint – readymix or powder
● acrylic paint as a base
● paintbrushes
● water jars
● felt pens
● colouring materials

67 Simple stick puppets

Scope
Animal puppets mounted on a stick or tube

Age
6–10

Organisation
6–7 year-olds: groups of 6–8;
8–10 year-olds: groups of up to 15 working individually

Time
1 1/2 hours

Cross-curricular links
English (stories)

You will need
sock for each child; newspaper;
PVA glue; felt and fabric pieces;
buttons; needles and thread;
stick or cardboard tube for each child;
masking tape; wool

Purposes
● To make a 3-D model.
● To tell a story, using puppets.

Activity
1 Demonstrate how to make an animal stick puppet:
– Stuff the stock with crumpled newspaper.

– Cut out eyes and ears from felt or fabric and stick these on.
– Add other features – nose, tongue, mane, etc.
– Push the stick or tube up the leg of the sock, then bind the cuff of the stock tightly to the stick using masking tape or wool.
2 Ask the children to make their own animal stick puppets.

Further activities
▶ Make **papier-mâché** heads from a ball of crumpled newspaper which has been attached to a stick, then covered with strips of pasted paper. Puppets heads made like this can then be painted and have fabric bodies attached.

▶ Read the children a story such as *Where the Wild Things Are* by Maurice Sendak. Ask them to make puppets to illustrate the story, then tell the story with their puppets.

68 Bottle people

Scope
Nativity figures made with papier-mâché over a bottle

Age
9–11

Organisation
Groups of up to 15 working individually

Time
3 hours in 3 sessions

Cross-curricular links
RE (Christmas – Nativity figures)

You will need
newspaper; newsprint;
bottle for each child ;
masking tape;
cellulose paste mix;
tissue paper (optional);
thick paint to mix flesh tones;
thick and fine paintbrushes;
water jars; card for arms;
fabrics for clothes;
staplers (optional);
needles and thread (optional); pins;
extra items such as sticks for
shepherd's crooks, as necessary

Purposes
● To make a 3-D figure for a Nativity scene.

Activity
Session 1
1 Demonstrate making the head and body of the Nativity bottle person:
– Crumple a sheet of newspaper (tabloid size) and place this in the centre of a second sheet.
– Enclose the crumpled ball of paper in the other sheet, keeping all the corners free and place this on the top of the bottle to form the head.
– Use masking tape to make a neck and to hold the head on the bottle body.
– Trim away some of the excess newspaper hanging down, and use masking tape to make sure the head is firmly fixed to the bottle.
– Show how to tear strips of newsprint. (Remind the children that the paper will tear easily into strips in one direction but not the other.)
– Using strips of paper covered with paste, cover the head and the body of the bottle person, overlapping the strips and smoothing them down as you work. Some children may like to add 3-D features to the faces with small pieces of tissue paper soaked in paste.
– Set the model aside to dry.
2 Ask the children to make their own Nativity bottle people.

Session 2
3 When the heads and bodies are dry, ask the children to paint the faces, necks and hair. Leave these to dry.

Session 3
4 Demonstrate how to dress the Nativity bottle person:
– Cut arms from thin card. (*See* below.)
– Cover the arms with fabric sleeves cut from a single piece of material.

– Stick the sleeves on, or attach with stapler or needle and thread.

– Drape the figure in material to clothe the body and pin this in position.

– Attach the arms to the shoulders at the back, using pins.

– Cut a square of material to make the shepherd's headdress and fix this with a dab of glue, adding a strip of material to tie round the head. Kings will need crowns or turbans.

– Add belts, cloaks, etc., as required.

5 Ask the children to dress their own Nativity bottle people.

Teaching points

▶ The baby for the Nativity scene can be made from a cardboard tube. The head is similar to that of the bottle people, but smaller. The head is painted, the baby wrapped in cloth. No arms are needed.

▶ Ask some children to make a stable from a large box; others could make sheep or angels. (These could be done as bottle people or *see* idea 83 for smaller angels.) In this way everyone in the class can contribute to the scene.

▶ If the figures are to be painted, not dressed in material, arms need to be added at the first stage when the head is stuck to the bottle. Roll a sheet of newspaper into a thin roll and use this for the arms (children will need help with this). Fix the newspaper roll firmly with masking tape to the back of the model at the shoulders, then trim to the correct size before 'bandaging' with paper-and-paste strips.

▶ This activity could be done with younger children if you are able to work with a small group, or have help in the classroom.

Further activities

▶ Bottle people could be used to illustrate characters from books.

69 Houses with gardens

Scope
Model houses with gardens made from boxes covered in papier-mâché

Age
5–10
(simplify instructions for 5–7 year-olds)

Organisation
Individual work;
5–7 year-olds: small groups;
9–11 year-olds: up to whole class if adequate space

Time
3 hours, time depending on ages of children and finish required (2 or 3 sessions)

Cross-curricular links
History, geography (houses and homes)

You will need
shoe box size cardboard box for each child;
larger shallower boxes or cardboard trays;
newspaper;
cellulose paste;
masking tape;
spare cardboard boxes for cutting up;
readymix or powder paints;
coloured papers (optional);
paintbrushes; water jars;
pictures of houses

Purpose

● To make a 3-D model covered in **papier-mâché**.

Activity

1 With the children, look at pictures of houses with pitched roofs, and any other distinguishing features, such as thatched rooves, timber beams, if you are studying Tudors.

2 Demonstrate making a model house, covered with papier-mâché:

– Shape the end of the box into a triangle to support a pitched roof (*see* diagram).

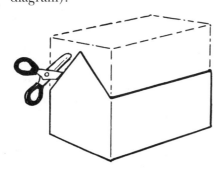

– If the boxes are not tall enough to do this, add a triangular piece of cardboard to each end to support the roof.

– Measure across the width of the box/roof, and down the sides of the triangle, to work out the size of the

rectangle for the roof (add a little extra to the measurements for roof overhang).

– Cut out the roof and place it in position, fixing securely with masking tape.

– Cover the house with strips of pasted newspaper (*see* idea 68).

– Leave the house to dry, before painting.

3 Ask the children to make their own papier-mâché covered cardboard houses.

Teaching points

▶ With older juniors, you could suggest ways to make the porch (a small open box is easiest), to add timbers and to achieve the effect of tiles or thatch. (Corrugated paper is one option – best stuck on after the pasting stage.)

▶ Once the houses are painted, show how a simple garden can be made in a flat cardboard tray. The children can create paths, areas of grass or vegetable gardens out of paper, paint, carpet or other materials.

Further activities

▶ With younger children, you could look at story books and recreate houses like those illustrated, for instance, *Tilly's House* by Faith Jacques, frog's garden from *Frog and Toad All Year* by Arnold Lobel.

70 Action figures

Scope
Papier-mâché figures made from rolled newspapers

Age
9–11

Organisation
Individual work; up to half a class (whole class with extra adult help)

Time
3 hours (2 or 3 sessions)

You will need
newspaper; cardboard tubes about 23 cm long for each child; masking tape (roll between 3 or 4 children); cellulose paste; thick paint; paintbrushes; water jars; tissue paper; wool; fabric scraps

Purpose
● To make 3-D **papier-mâché** figures which can be posed in different positions.

Activity
1 Demonstrate making a papier-mâché action figure:

– Make the head as for bottle people in idea 68, but twist the ends of the wrapping sheet around, then push them into the end of the cardboard tube.

– Secure this with masking tape.

– Roll up a double sheet of newspaper as tightly as possible to make stiff tubes for the arms and legs. (Children may find this difficult and can work with a partner at this stage.)

– Secure the rolled tubes with masking tape in a few places.

– Take one of the rolled tubes and place it across the back of the model under the head to make the shoulders and arms, securing it with two diagonal strips of masking tape.

– Take the second rolled tube, bend it in the middle and push the bent end into the end of the tube to form legs.

– Trim the limbs if they seem too long, and bend them at the elbows and knees, wrists and ankles.

– Use tape to join the hands if you like.

– Take strips of newspaper and paste and

'bandage' the figure all over, smoothing down the strips as you work.

– When the figure is damp you will be able to manipulate it into a more realistic position.

– Prop it up to dry, where it can be left undisturbed for several days.

– When the figure is dry, it can be painted and decorated. Usually the position suggests what the character could become.

2 Ask the children to make their own papier-mâché action figures.

Teaching points
▶ You would be well advised to try this activity for yourself before demonstrating to the children. You could then have one half-finished figure to give them the idea of what they are aiming at.

▶ It is important that the children learn to smooth down the pasted paper layers as they work. The finished work will look very rough if this is not done.

▶ Talk to the children about the sort of activities that produce interesting poses – a dancer, someone throwing a javelin, etc. – and about where the body bends. If they are not sure about a position, allow them to pose for one another.

Further activities
▶ Look at sculptures of figures in your local art gallery or in books.

71 Papier-mâché bowls

Scope
Bowls made in a mould, decorated with torn paper collages

Age
8–11 (see note in Teaching points on amending the activity for 5–7 year-olds)

Organisation
Individual work in whole class

Time
2 hours (3 sessions)

Purpose
● To make and decorate a bowl, using a pre-formed mould.

Activity
Session 1
1 Demonstrate making bowls in a mould:

– Explain that you will be using a china or glass bowl as a mould, but that you do not want the **papier-mâché** bowl to stick to it.

– Grease the mould well with Vaseline or line it with cling film.

– If you grease the mould, line it with some unpasted strips of newspaper.

– Take some short strips of newspaper, paste them all over and lay them in the

mould, overlapping a little. Work all round the bowl.

– Leave the paper extending over the edges of the bowl and either trim the edge at a later stage or leave an interesting frilly edge.

– Cover the first layer with a layer of tinted paper.

– Repeat this process three times more so that the bowl has a total of eight layers plus overlaps.

– Decorate the inside of the bowl with a torn paper **collage**, using coloured pages from the inside pages of colour supplements. (Avoid very glossy pages as they do not absorb the paste well.)

2 Ask the children to make their own bowls in moulds.

Session 2

3 Leave the bowls to dry for several days, then ease them out of the moulds. If you have used Vaseline, peel the first, greasy layer of paper off the base.

4 Decorate the bottoms of the bowls with torn paper collage work to complement the inside of the bowls.

Session 3

5 Allow the collage work to dry, then finish off the bowls by varnishing them with diluted PVA glue.

Teaching points

▶ I encourage children to apply paste with their fingers, but you may prefer them to use brushes. In either case, the paper should be pasted all over but not swimming in paste.

▶ The paper should be smoothed down well, especially the coloured top layer.

▶ It might be easier to provide 5–7 year-olds with a polystyrene disposable dish that they can line with paper, then decorate, leaving the dish in place to support the papier-mâché work.

▶ Older children could add bases to their bowls once they have been removed from the moulds, using circles of card, attached to the bottom of the bowls with masking tape. They then paste strips of newspaper over the card to strengthen the base which they decorate to go with the rest of the bowl.

72 3-D fish

Scope
Decorative fish made from card and papier-mâché

Age
9–11

Organisation
Individual work;
structures: small groups;
papier-mâché stage: whole class

Time
2 1/2–3 hours (2 sessions)

You will need
copies of pcm 72 on card for each child;
stiff cardboard from cardboard cartons;
newspaper; masking tape; newsprint;
cellulose paste; paints: powder paint or
acrylic for base, readymix paints for
decoration; PVA glue for varnishing
books on tropical fish

pcm 72 on page 90

Purpose
● To make a 3-D structure covered in **papier-mâché**.

Activity
Session 1

1 With the children, look at pictures of tropical fish for ideas for patterns to decorate your fish.

2 Demonstrate constructing a 3-D fish:
– Cut two identical fish shapes and the gusset, from stiff card, using templates cut from pcm 72.
– Tape the tops of the two fish shapes together.
– Crumple up a small piece of newspaper and insert this in between the two fish shapes to hold them apart at the base.
– Tape the gusset into position around the base of the fish, using small pieces of tape.

– Paste strips of newsprint all over the fish, paying particular attention to the edges.
– Leave to dry.

3 Ask the children to make their own fish.

Session 2

4 The children paint their fish.

Teaching points

▶ It is best to be on hand to help the children make the actual fish shapes, so working with a small group is best at this stage.

Further activities

▶ After making a fish with the templates provided, the children could be challenged to design their own fish or other animal, such as a cat lying down (legs are difficult).

73 Large 3-D landscapes

Scope
Landscapes made out of papier-mâché

Age
5–11

Organisation
Groups of 4 working on one landscape

Time
Making land: 1 1/2 hours; painting time: 1 hour (2 sessions)

Cross-curricular links
Geography, English (stories)

You will need
large sheets of strong cardboard cut from carton, or sheet of hardboard; newspaper; cellulose paste; masking tape; powder paints; paintbrushes; water jars

Purpose
● To make a 3-D landscape out of **papier-mâché**.

Activity
Session 1
1 Demonstrate how to make the papier-mâché landscape:
– Crumple up some sheets of newspaper to make hills and stick these on to the base with masking tape.
– Tear strips of paper and paste these over the hills and board. Paste about four layers over everything, changing the direction that you lay the strips in. The shapes of the hills can be moulded a little while the model is damp.
2 Ask the children to make their own landscapes, working in groups of four.
3 Leave the models to dry for several days.

Session 2
The children paint the landscapes.

Further activities
▶ 9–11 year-olds might be asked to link this to geography and create specific landscapes.
▶ Children could make small model houses and other buildings to place on the landscape. (A pattern for a basic model house is given on the pcm for idea 76. Older children could make their own patterns up after trying out the set pattern.)
▶ Children could create an arctic landscape or snow scene. (Make icebergs using crumpled cereal boxes as a base to paste the paper over.)
▶ Landscapes to go with stories such as the dump in *Stig of the Dump* by Clive King would be an exciting project.

74 Bas-relief faces

Scope
Making 3-D faces, using papier-mâché over Plasticine

Age
8–11

Organisation
Individual work in whole class

Time
Papier-mâché work: 1 1/2 hours; painting time: 1 hour (2 sessions)

Cross-curricular links
Geography (study of other cultures and countries)

You will need
sheet of strong cardboard approximately 15 cm by 20 cm for each child, cut from carton; Plasticine; newspaper; cellulose paste; paints; paint brushes; water jars; fabric; raffia; wool; feathers; dried pasta

Purpose
● To make a 3-D **papier-mâché** face or mask, modelling the features.

Activity
Session 1
1 With the children, look at pictures of masks from different cultures and countries. Discuss their uses in other cultures.
2 Demonstrate making the 3-D face:
– Mould the features from Plasticine and press them on to the card to make a **bas-relief** face.
– Apply strips of pasted paper over these, overlapping the strips.
– Cover the whole card with several layers of pasted paper.
3 Ask the children to make their own bas-relief faces.

Session 2
4 When the masks are thoroughly dry, they can be painted, and perhaps decorated further with other materials such as fabric, raffia, wool or feathers. Dried pasta might also be stuck on before painting.

Teaching points
▶ The masks can be as natural or fantastic as you like, depending on what you have been studying, and the criteria you set the children.
▶ Instead of using Plasticine, you could build up features with a 'mash' of paper, but this is hard to make in large quantities.

Further activities
▶ 10–11 year-olds could study coins showing bas-relief profiles and make their own bas-relief profiles on a larger scale.

75 Model mummy case

Scope
Group project, using papier-mâché linked to work on the Egyptians

Age
9–11

Organisation
Groups of 3 or 4 working on one model

Time
3–4 hours (3 sessions)

Cross-curricular links
History (Egyptians)

You will need
large strong cardboard cartons; masking tape; newspaper and plain newsprint; cellulose paste; Plasticine; paints; paintbrushes; water jars; foil paper (optional); books on Egyptians or pictures of mummy cases

Purpose
● To make a 3-D **papier-mâché** model of a mummy case.

Activity
Session 1
1 With the children, look at pictures of mummy cases, real ones if you are able to visit a suitable museum.
2 Get the children to make sketches of these.

Session 2
3 Discuss how to make a basic mummy case shape out of sheets of cardboard carton. (Half-size, that is about 100 cm long, would be a good size to aim for.) The children may need help with this but encourage them to discuss how it might be done and have a go for themselves.

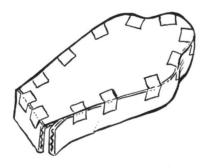

4 Show them how to tape the structure together with masking tape.

5 Demonstrate tearing strips of newspaper and covering the model with pasted strips of paper, overlapping the strips.
6 The children cover their own models with strips of pasted paper. These need to be covered with about three layers, finishing with a layer of plain newsprint.
7 Dry the mummy cases thoroughly before painting.

Session 3
8 The children paint their models. Discuss with them the colours available to the Egyptians and ask them to try to keep to this range of colours. (Information on this can be found in books on the Egyptians.)

Further activities
► A mummy to go with the mummy case could be made from a cardboard mummy shape covered with crumpled paper and tape which is then bound with strips of sheeting.
► Other papier-mâché projects linked to the Egyptians could be making mummified cat and raven forms using crumpled paper bound with tape into the appropriate shapes.
► Jars for body organs could be made over pots and jars with the appropriate god's head on top of the jar.

76 Small model houses

Scope
Small model houses made from a pattern

Age
6–11

Organisation
Individual work suitable for whole class, depending on age

Time
1 1/2 hours

Cross-curricular links
History, geography (houses and homes); Maths (nets)

You will need
copies of pcm 76 on card for each child; sheets of card for each child if pcm is on paper; glue; coloured pencils

pcm 76 on page 91

Purpose
● To make a simple 3-D model from a net.

Activity
1 With the children, look at pictures of numerous different houses and talk about the different types of doors, windows, roofing materials etc., used.
2 Demonstrate making the model houses:
– Stick the pcm on to card if not copied on card.
– Cut out the house and fold along the dotted lines (older children could be taught to score these lines using a ruler and scissors but the glue needs to be dry before they do this).
– Show how the house is formed, then flatten it out again and draw on and colour windows, roof tiles and other features. (Remind the children which is the bottom of the building.)
3 The children make and colour their own model houses.
4 When the features have been drawn on and coloured, the children fold their houses into shape and stick them together.

Further activities
► Once they have made the basic house, 9–11 year-olds could be asked to develop their own pattern for a house of a different shape.
► The houses could be arranged on a base of paper and a village made. Adapt the pattern if you want to make a village from the Middle Ages.

77 Model figures

pcm 77 on page 92

Scope
Card figures made with moveable joints

Age
5–10

Organisation
Individual work suitable for whole class (8–10 year-olds), or small groups (5–7 year-olds)

Time
2 hours

Cross-curricular links
English (stories), PE (movement), Geography (Chinese shadow puppets)

You will need
copies of pcm 77 on thin card for each child; A4 sheets of card for each child if pcm is on paper; colouring materials; coloured paper; glue; brass paper fasteners, 8 per child; wool (optional); books on puppetry or the Far East (optional)

Purpose
● To make an articulated figure to illustrate a story.

Activity
1 Demonstrate making a model figure:
– Cut out the model from pcm 77 and decorate it, or have one cut-out and partly decorated, ready to assemble in front of the children.
– Join the arms at the shoulders and elbows, and the legs at the hips and knees, with brass paper fasteners.
2 Ask the children to cut out and decorate, then assemble their own models.

Teaching points
▶ Encourage the children to make their figures as individual as possible, even though they are all starting from the same basic pattern. They can add clothes in different styles, perhaps using coloured papers and glue, wool for hair, etc. Stress that you would like all the figures to end up very different from each other.

▶ You may like the children to draw their figures first, specifying that they are to draw either a character from a book, a person who works in a circus or even themselves in a special outfit.

▶ This activity is only suitable for small groups of 5–7 year-olds who can cut out fairly accurately. Children of this age will need help when using the paper fasteners.

Further activities
▶ If you are studying puppetry or Chinese culture, you could adapt this idea to make silhouette shadow puppets mounted on thin garden canes. Refer to books on puppetry or on the Far East for ideas, and with the children look at the intricate outlines of the puppets. These could be made of dark card and would not need colouring.

78 Model birds

Scope
Bird models, using cardboard tubes as bodies

Age
8–11

Organisation
Individual work in whole class

Time
1 1/2–2 hours

Cross-curricular links
Science (birds), Geography (rainforest)

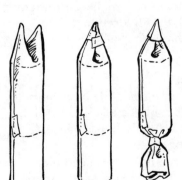

Purpose
● To make a 3-D model.

Activity
1 With the children, look at pictures of birds, particularly the way that the feathers overlap each other on the wings. Look at pictures of tropical birds if doing work on the rainforest.
2 In advance, try out making a model bird:
– Lay the cardboard tube lengthwise on a sheet of A4 coloured paper, leaving about 7 cm of paper at one end (this will form the head and beak), and about 11 cm at the other end which will form the tail.
– Roll the paper around the tube and stick it down.
– To make the head, hold the 'body' in both hands, and press in on both sides of the head end, making the paper into a V

shape. Then fold this V of paper under to make a point which will be the beak and tape this into position.
– Cover this with a small triangle of yellow paper.
– Press the other end of the paper in around the cardboard tube, like a Christmas cracker, to make the start of the tail.
– Either snip this into 'feathers' or add torn or cut paper feathers to make the tail.
– Cut out the wings.

– Decorate the wings before sticking them into position. If you cover them with paper feathers, cut lots of feathers at once from folded paper. Start sticking the feathers at the tips of the wings first and overlap them, working towards the centre.

– When the wings are decorated, stick them on to the body.

– Add eyes and pipe-cleaner legs and feet to finish off the bird. (If you don't have pipe cleaners, cut legs and feet from card.)

3 Demonstrate the above stages to the children. Show them the model you made earlier so that they know what they are aiming at.

4 Ask the children to make their own model birds.

Teaching points

▶ Some children will need help forming the V shape which becomes the head and beak.

▶ Stress that you expect all the birds to be different and individual, although they are all starting from the same basic shape. They can be as realistic or as fanciful as they like.

▶ Feathers torn from sugar paper can be very effective and curl well.

▶ Encourage the children to try to see the models as designs as they are working on them: for instance, if they have done elaborate multi-coloured wings, how can they make the rest of the bird go with this? By adding some similar feathers to the tail perhaps?

79 Model insects

Purpose
● To make a 3-D model.

Activity
Session 1

1 With the children, look at pictures of all sorts of insects. Discuss the enormous variety of insects that there are.

2 In advance, try out making a model insect:

– Make a head first by crumpling up a small sheet of newspaper and placing this in the centre of a second sheet.

– Draw the corners of this sheet together, to make a sort of 'tail'.

Twist these ends round, and insert them into the end of the cardboard tube, to make a head coming out of a body.

– Stick this on with masking tape.

– Add wings, made from a folded piece of card.

– Make legs, antennae, etc., using the materials you have.

3 Demonstrate the above stages to the children. Show them the model you made earlier so they know what they are aiming at.

4 Ask the children to make their own model insects and leave the glue to dry.

Session 2

5 The children paint their insects.

Teaching points

▶ Children who want to use cellophane and other materials such as soft sheets of polystyrene packaging for wings could stick these on after the bodies, etc., have been painted.

▶ You could ask the children to cover the heads and bodies with layers of **papier-mâché** before the wings are added and the models finished off. This would mean doing the project in three stages.

Further activities

▶ With older children, work on insects could focus on camouflage. Using leaf shapes for wings (supply lots of interesting ones as templates), get children to invent 3-D insects using card. Mount these on larger leaves of similar shape and colour. This work would link with work on tropical rainforests.

80 Animal sculptures

Scope
Sculptures made from plaster bandage over armatures

Age
8–11

Organisation
Making armatures: individuals or pairs in whole class; plaster bandage stage: small groups in a specially prepared 'wet' area

Time
3–4 hours (3 sessions)

Cross-curricular links
History (Egyptians), Science (animals)

You will need
stiff card; cardboard rolls; newspaper; plastic bottles; other junk materials masking tape (roll between 3 or 4); rolls of plaster bandage; containers of water such as ice cream cartons to dip the bandages in; readymix paint; paint brushes; water jars; wool; glue

Purpose
- To learn one of the processes of making a sculpture.

Activity

Session 1

1 Talk about the type of animal it is feasible to make, using this technique. For example, making a standing giraffe would be extremely difficult but an animal with thicker legs is quite possible. Different shaped plastic bottles may provide good 'starter' shapes: a long, fat lemonade bottle might become a dolphin with cardboard additions for fins and a tail and to alter the shape of its nose; a short fat bottle might become a pig.

2 Demonstrate how to make a basic animal shape (**armature**) with card and other junk materials. Make stiff rolls of several layers of newspaper to use for legs, necks, etc. and crumpled balls of newspaper for softer, rounder shapes. (You could make an armature in advance to show the children what to aim at.)

3 Ask the children, working individually or in pairs, to make their own animal shapes.

Session 2

4 Demonstrate how to cover the armature with strips of plaster bandage which have been dipped in water:
– Start in one area of the animal and wrap the bandage exactly as if you were bandaging a limb.

– Then work on an adjacent area, overlapping the bandage a bit.
– Smooth the ends of the plaster bandage down well while it is still wet.
– Form bits of the bandage into small lumps for noses, etc., and add these while the model is wet.
– When the model is done, set aside to dry well for about 24 hours.

5 Ask the children, working in small groups in a specially prepared 'wet' area, to cover their animal armatures with plaster bandage.

Session 3

6 When the models are dry, ask the children to paint them and finish them off with other materials, if necessary.

Teaching points

▶ Do try out this medium for yourself first if you have never used it. It is easy to use, but a bit messy. Clean up with a damp cloth to avoid inhaling dust.

▶ Cut up bandage in advance in 50 cm lengths. The children then cut this into smaller strips.

Further activities

▶ If the children are studying the Egyptians, they could produce 'mummified' cats and ravens. Make the armatures out of crumpled newspapers bound into shape with masking tape.

▶ Look at sculptures in your local art gallery or in books. Talk about how they have been made.

 # 81 Scarecrows

Scope
Life-size stuffed figures: soft sculptures

Age
5–7

Organisation
Groups of 5 or 6, working with an adult

Time
1 1/2 hours

Cross-curricular links
English (poems, stories), Geography (farming)

Purpose
- To make a large soft sculpture.

Activity

1 Discuss what scarecrows are for and how you plan to make one. Ask the children for ideas about how to make it, or about its character.

2 Working with a group of children, make the scarecrow:
– Set the children to stuffing both legs and body of the pair of tights with crumpled newspaper.

– When full, tie this up at the top. It will become the arms, neck and head of the scarecrow.
– Dress the arms in a blouse or jumper, leaving the body of the tights at the top for the head and neck.
– Squeeze these into shape and tie as necessary, or tape with masking tape.
– Ask one child to make a face mask from thin card and paint it.
– Ask another child to cut out a pair of hands from thin card.

You will need

newspaper; old pairs of tights; old clothes, adult or child-sized, but not a mixture of both; masking tape; thin card; paints; paintbrushes; water jars; needles and thread; wool

– Choose the rest of the clothes you need: if you are making a female scarecrow, you could stuff another pair of tights to form the legs and pelvis and join this on to the jumper or blouse with tacking stitches, after the chest has been stuffed.

– If you are making a male scarecrow, tack a pair of trousers on to the shirt or jumper, then stuff this whole body area and the legs, tying the bottom of the trousers when you finish.

– If you can, borrow a pair of wellingtons to finish off the legs.

– Attach the mask to the face and the hands to the arms.

– Make hair from wool.

– Add a hat if you can get hold of one.

– Now have fun sitting the scarecrow on a chair in a position that you all approve of. If the scarecrow seems to have a particular character, consider this as you arrange the pose. You may have to be a bit brutal, tying him or her to the chair if necessary to keep the position.

– Add any accessories that seem to be needed – a bandana handkerchief or even a cup of tea or a newspaper to read!

Further activities

► Make several friends for the first character, or even a whole family. The children could write poems and make up stories about them.

► If you can get hold of some dressing-up clothes and pieces of cloth, the children might make some people in historical costumes.

82 Model snowmen

Scope

Simple snowmen models made over a jar

Age

5–9

Organisation

Individual work;
5–7 year-olds: groups of 6;
8–9 year-olds: up to half class

Time

1 1/2 hours

Cross-curricular links

RE (Christmas),
Science (seasons – winter),
English (poems)

You will need

newspaper;
jam jar or plastic container with wide neck for each child;
PVA glue;
rolls of cotton wool;
strips of different coloured fabric approximately 40 cm by 3 cm;
coloured paper for features, etc.;
yogurt pots for hats

Purpose

● To make a simple 3-D model.

Activity

1 Demonstrate making a snowman model:

– Crumple a single sheet of tabloid-sized newspaper into a ball.

– Enclose this in another sheet, leaving the ends of the second sheet hanging out. This will be the head and the neck of the snowman.

– Put some glue round the inside neck of the jar and insert the dangling bits of newspaper into it to fix the head.

– Cover the head and jar with dabs of glue and wrap 'sheets' of cotton wool (peeled off a roll) around the head and body to cover it.

– Tie a strip of fabric around the neck tightly, to separate the head and body.

2 Ask the children to make their own model snowmen.

3 At this stage the snowmen will look rather alike. Suggest the children add features, buttons and hats to make the models more individual.

Teaching points

► It is cheapest to use large rolls of cotton wool and to unwrap some of the separate layers to offer the children.

83 Christmas angels

Scope
Small models made from a basic pattern

Age
8–11

Organisation
Individual work in whole class

Time
11/2 hours

You will need
copies of pcm 83 on thin card for each child; A4 thin white or pastel coloured card if pcm is on paper; glue; Sellotape; pressed cotton wool balls for the heads, 2 1/2 cm in diameter; pipe cleaners, half per model; black felt pens; small pieces of gold and silver foil paper or card; scraps of lace, sequins, doilies, etc.; wool

pcm 83 on page 93

Purpose
● To make a 3-D model figure.

Activity
1 Demonstrate making a Christmas angel:

– Put a dab of glue on one end of the piece of pipe cleaner and insert this into the hole in the cotton wool ball. This will be the angel's neck.

– Draw a face on one side of this head and stick wool hair on to it. Set this aside for the glue to dry while you make the body.

– Cut out the body of the angel from pcm 83 and fold it round to make a cone.

– Cut out the arms and attach these to the back of the body, using a dab of glue.

– Attach the head by pushing the pipe cleaner down the small hole at the top of the cone.

– Stick this with a small piece of Sellotape inside the cone/body.

– Finish off the angel with the halo, using gold or silver foil, and wings. (Decorate the wings before attaching them to the body.) Decorate the angel with scraps of lace, sequins, etc.

2 Ask the children to make their own angel models.

Teaching points
▶ Emphasise that all the angels should be as individual as the children can make them. They can add musical instruments if they like, too.

84 Christmas wreaths

Scope
Wreaths made from stuffed paper covered in paper leaves and flowers

Age
5–11

Organisation
5–8 year-olds:
groups of 5 or 6 making wreath;
9–11 year-olds:
individual work in whole class

Time
Groups: 1 hour;
individual work: 1 1/2 hours

Cross-curricular links
RE (festivals, Christmas)

You will need
newspaper; masking tape; brown tissue paper; different green papers; red paper; foil; small bits of tinsel; glue; variety of pressed or fresh leaves

Purpose
● To make a decorative 3-D wreath.

Activity
1 Demonstrate making a Christmas wreath:

– Loosely crumple into a long sausage shape a large sheet of broadsheet newspaper.

– Twist this around into a circular wreath shape and tape the ends together with masking tape.

– Bind this loosely with brown tissue paper, gluing it into place with dabs of glue.

– Cut out some leaves, using real leaves as templates, and stick them on the wreath.

– Roll some 'berries' out of small pieces of red tissue paper and stick these on, too.

2 Ask the children to start making their own wreaths.

3 Have a break and demonstrate how to make a flower. (*See* idea 30. You could use the pcm or make your own flowers.) A poinsettia can easily be made with six red petals and a small bit of gold tinsel in the centre.

4 Ask the children to make their own flowers and add them to the wreath.

Teaching points
▶ The more full of leaves they are, the nicer the wreaths look. Several layers of leaves can be cut at once from tissue paper. Providing a good range of papers allows a discussion of the contrasts that these different qualities of paper provide in the wreath.

▶ Younger children will probably need help making the basic wreath shape, but even children who are poor at cutting out should be able to contribute leaves that are useable and roll 'berries' out of tissue paper.

Clay work

See pcm on page 81 for examples of clay work

The activities in this section aim to teach the basic skills necessary for clay work at primary level. In common with other areas of primary art, there are two strands running through all the activities suggested: the teaching and learning of the *craft*, and the opportunity for *self-expression*. Activities for children of this age should always balance these two elements.

The main skills to teach at primary level are:

- Modelling with clay: through modelling, children learn about the qualities of clay while expressing themselves in this wonderfully tactile medium.
- Making secure joints, using **slip**.
- Finishing off the work well.
- **Wedging** the clay to expel air bubbles.
- Making thumb pots.
- Making **impressions** in the clay, using a variety of implements.

- Rolling coils of clay.
- Rolling slabs of clay (from eight years onwards).

All these skills are covered in the activities in this section.

Firing and finishing off work

In Year 1, all work does not need to be **fired**. The experience of working in clay is valuable in itself. It is not necessary to **glaze-fire** everything at primary level. Often **biscuit-firing**, followed by painting, is suitable for decorative pieces, giving the children the opportunity for self-expression as they paint their models. Painted models can then be varnished by dipping them in a small bath of diluted PVA glue. (Dipping is more successful than painting on varnish as there is less risk of smudging.) I would offer nine- to eleven-year-olds the opportunity to have a piece of their work glazed if it were something that could be used at home.

Basic equipment

Depending on activity select from:
- wire-ended tools for scooping excess clay from backs of models
- wooden boards to work on and to dry work on
- pots of slip
- stiff paint brushes

- old table knives
- cheese-type wire cutters for clay (useful but not essential)
- needle-type cutters for clay (can be made by pushing tapestry needles into corks)
- extruding tools

For rolling slabs of clay you will need:
- cloths (any natural fibre) approximately half tea-towel size
- wooden rolling pins
- pairs of sticks approximately 1 cm deep to roll clay between

Much equipment can be improvised if money is short, for instance:
- wooden lolly sticks – good small modelling tools
- junk materials for making impressions – old biro casings, wooden clothes pegs

and the springs from them, kitchen forks
- old spoons for scooping excess clay from back of work

(You only need enough equipment for a group of children, not the whole class.)

85 Birds and faces

Scope
Simple unfired clay projects

Age
5–6

Organisation
Groups of 6–8, working individually

Time
1 hour

Cross-curricular links
Science (birds, seasons), PSE (faces, ourselves)

You will need
clay; wooden boards; cutting tools (*see* Introduction to Clay work, p.63); feathers; dried beans; pasta; buttons; small sticks

Purpose
● To provide experiences of modelling clay, combined with other materials.

Activity
1 Demonstrate **wedging** the clay. (Although this work will not be **fired**, this is a basic technique that needs to be learned.)
2 Talk about some of the things the children might like to make, using the materials supplied, such as exotic and unusual birds, or faces.
3 Ask the children to make their models.

Teaching points
▶ This activity provides an opportunity for young children to experiment with clay without getting bogged down prematurely in learning techniques or producing 'proper pots'. *This play stage of discovery is a very important one and should not be rushed.*

86 Nests with eggs

Scope
Making thumb-pots and rolling balls of clay

Age
5–7

Organisation
Groups of 6–8, working individually

Time
3/4 hour

Cross-curricular links
Science (spring, life cycle of birds)

You will need
clay; wooden boards; simple tools to make textures with (*see* Introduction to Clay work, p.63); paints; bird books or pictures of birds

Purposes
● To make a first thumb-pot.
● To practise rolling balls of clay.

Activity
1 Demonstrate how to make a thumb-pot:
– Make a small ball of clay.
– Press your thumb into the centre.
– Keeping your thumb in the centre, move the ball round while pressing your thumb against the clay. This will form a bowl with a thick wall.
– Work round the bowl again to make the wall of the bowl thinner. (This pot could be refined greatly with older children but for this activity leave it fairly thick.)

– Texture the outside of the nest, using tools.
2 Invite the children to make their own thumb-pot birds' nests.
3 Ask them to make birds' eggs from small balls of clay and stick them in the nest with **slip**.
4 Remind them to mark their initials on the base of the nests.
5 Leave the nests to dry, then **biscuit-fire** them.
6 The children paint the nests and eggs, perhaps referring to bird books.

Teaching points
▶ Look at real nests with the children if possible or, failing this, at pictures of birds and nests.

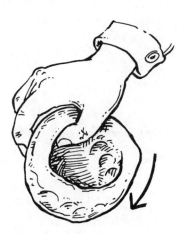

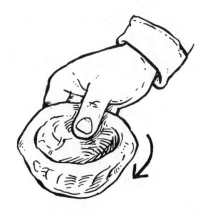

87 Tortoises

Scope
Simple project for teaching some basic techniques

Age
5–7

Organisation
Groups of 6–8, working individually

Time
1 hour

Cross-curricular links
Science (pets, zoos)

You will need
clay; wooden boards; simple tools for impressing patterns (*see* Introduction to Clay work, p.63); blunt knifes; pots of slip; paints; glaze

Purpose
● To give practise in basic techniques: rolling a ball of clay, rolling coils, making **impressed patterns**.

Activity
1 Demonstrate how to make a clay tortoise:
– Roll a ball of clay and flatten it out on one side for the tortoise's body.
– Roll some more clay into coils or thin sausages and cut these into four equal pieces for the legs.
– Roll another small coil to make the neck and head.
– Join the legs, then the head, on to the body, using **slip** and making sure you get rid of the cracks along the joints.
– Mark two eyes on the head.
2 Ask the children to make their own tortoises.
3 Remind the children to mark their initials on the underside of their models, preferably before they pattern the shells.
4 Then, with the children, try out some impressed patterns for the tortoises' shells on spare clay. Discuss which of these would be most effective, then ask them to pattern their shells.

impressed patterns

5 Leave the tortoises to dry, then **biscuit-fire** them.
6 The children paint their tortoises, or they can be glazed and **fired** a second time.

Teaching points
▶ It is best to remove your tortoise at the patterning stage so the children don't try to reproduce it exactly.

Further activities
▶ Small hedgehogs are another simple project to do with children at this stage. The head and body can be formed from one lump of clay. The bodies can then be textured to represent bristles. Show the children how to scoop out some of the clay from underneath the bodies with a small spoon or looped tool before texturing the hedgehogs.

88 Owls

Scope
Small clay models textured with feather patterns

Age
5–7

Organisation
Groups of 6–8 working individually

Time
1 hour

Cross-curricular links
English (stories), Science (birds)

You will need
clay; wooden boards; tools to make impressions with (*see* Introduction to Clay work, p.63) pots of slip; small wooden rolling pins; cloths; old table knives; paints (optional)

Purpose
● To practise some basic clay techniques.

Activity
1 Demonstrate how to make an owl's basic shape:
– Make a ball of clay, then roll this until it becomes an ovoid.
– Stand this on its end and press it firmly down on the board.
– Mark your initials on the base and at the same time push a pointed tool up through the centre of the body to help the clay dry out.
2 Ask the children to make their own basic owl shape and remind them to mark their initials on the base.
3 Now show the children how to roll out small pieces of clay with a rolling pin on a cloth, or flatten them with their hands.

4 Show them how to cut a wing shape from this flat sheet of clay and to see if this fits their owl.
5 When they have the shape and size of wing they like, show them how to use the first as a template for the second.
6 Show the children how to stick the wings to the sides of the owl's body, using **slip**, and to smooth out the joints at the top of the wings.
7 Suggest that they make impressions on scrap clay to try out various feather effects, then mark feathers on their owls.
8 Suggest they press eyes into the head.
9 They can cut claws from small scraps of rolled clay and stick these to the owl's base, using slip. (Omit claws if you think this is too complex.)
10 Dry the owls, then **fire** them. The children can decorate them as they wish.

Teaching points
▶ Look at pictures of owls with the children and show how their eyes look large because of the surrounding feathers. Talk about the textures of the feathers.

▶ Read stories about owls, such as *The Owl Who Was Afraid of the Dark* by C. Allan *et al.* or *Owl at Home* by Arnold Lobel.

Further activities
▶ Small penguins would be another simple animal form to make in a similar way.

89 Grotesque faces

Scope
Making grotesque faces from clay

Age
5–11

Organisation
Individual work in groups, size according to age of children

Time
1 hour

Cross-curricular links
English (stories – trolls, etc.)
History (gargoyles in local churches)

You will need
clay (stoneware clay for gargoyles); wooden boards; tools to make impressions with (*see* Introduction to Clay work, p.63) spoons or tools with wire loop for scooping out excess clay; pots of slip; metal sieve for older children (optional); paints; glaze

Purposes
● To model a 3-D form from clay.
● To make secure joints in clay, using tools.

Activity
1 Read stories or poems about monsters or trolls, such as 'The Three Billy Goats Gruff', or look at gargoyles in local churches.

2 Demonstrate how to make a grotesque face:
– **Wedge** the lump of clay, then pat it into a ball shape.
– Press two eye sockets into the 'face'.
– Turn the 'face' over, scoop out some clay from the centre of the back and smooth down.
– Mark your initials on the back and make a screw-sized hole near the top to hang it up.

– Turn the 'face' back and, using some **slip**, add a nose, smoothing away all signs of the joint.
– Cut a mouth in the clay.
– Add ears, again smoothing away the joints.
3 Put your model aside and ask the children to make their own grotesque faces.
4 Once they have made the basic face shape, ask the children to suggest ways to achieve the effect of hair, stubbly chins, eyes, etc. Ask them to try out some of their suggestions on spare clay so that they can see the effect before carrying them out on their models. Older children might enjoy making hair by pushing clay through a metal sieve.
5 After **biscuit-firing**, the faces can be painted, then varnished. Gargoyles inspired by church carvings would be best made of **stoneware clay** and left unpainted and unglazed.

Teaching points
▶ Unless you do clay work regularly, you will need to remind the children frequently to use slip to make good joints, smoothing the clay down well.
▶ These heads are sculptures and much of the artistic interest will come from contrasts of texture and shadow. Discuss these aspects with individual children as their work progresses.
▶ Encourage children to try out effects on pieces of scrap clay.
▶ Many children will need help scooping out excess clay from the back of the ball.

90 Crocodile-type monsters

Scope
Imaginative project for practising several techniques

Age
8–11

Organisation
Up to half class, depending on space and equipment, working individually

Time
1 1/2 hours

Cross-curricular links
English (myths and legends), Science (life-cycles of dinosaurs, crocodiles, etc.)

You will need
clay; wooden boards; tools to make impressions with (*see* Introduction to Clay work, p.63); pots of slip; old table knives; paints; glaze

Purposes

● To make an imaginative 3-D creature.
● To practise several important clay techniques.

Activity

1 Demonstrate making the crocodile monster:
– To make the head and body, **wedge** a lump of clay as big as a woman's fist.
– Roll it into a ball, then into a fat sausage.
– Continue rolling, pressing harder on each end until you have a long fat coil which is tapered at both ends.
– Roll another lump of clay half as big as the first into a thick coil and cut it into four equal pieces for the legs.
– Attach the legs to the body, using slip.
– Make a slit for the mouth in the head end.
– Turn the monster over, mark your initials on the underside, making sure at the same time that the legs are joined to the body.
– With a pencil or something similar, press some holes into the underside of the body to help it dry out.

2 On some spare clay, show how the tools make different **impressions** suitable for scales, etc.
3 Put your model away and ask the children to make their own crocodile monsters.
4 The children work on their models and add eyes, fins, spines and anything else they think the monster needs.
5 Fire the monsters when they are thoroughly dry. They may be painted or glazed as preferred.

Teaching points

▶ It is best to leave the monsters lying on their stomachs with their legs sticking out at the sides like a crocodile. However, children more experienced in clay work can make their monsters stand up on their legs, if the legs are not too thin. If necessary, support the weight of the body with a prop of some kind as the clay dries.

Further activities

▶ Look a the life-cycle of dinosaurs and crocodiles or dragons with the children. Ask them to make or draw the baby form of their monsters.

91 Decorative fish plaques

Scope
Rolled clay work decorated with impressions

Age
8–11

Organisation
Up to half a class depending on equipment available, working individually

Time
Making plaque: 1–11/2 hours; painting and varnishing: 1 hour

You will need
copies of pcm 91 preferably on card; clay; wooden boards; tools to make impressions with (*see* Introduction to Clay work, p.63); rolling pins; cloths; pairs of sticks; pots of slip; clay cutters (needle type); paints; glaze; paper

pcm 91 on page 94

Purposes
● To practise rolling slabs of clay.
● To explore making patterns in clay.

Activity
1 Demonstrate making a fish plaque:
– **Wedge** a lump of clay about as big as a woman's fist.
– Roll this into a ball, place it on the spread-out cloth and flatten it with your hands.
– Lay the sticks one either side of the clay, then roll the clay out flat with the rolling pin. (The sticks will ensure that the clay is rolled to an even thickness.)
– Cut out the fish shape from pcm 91, place the pattern on the clay and cut around it.
– Mark your initials on the reverse of the fish, then transfer it to a wooden board.
– Smooth the cut edges of the fish, so they will not be sharp when **fired**.
– Decorate the fish by pressing rows of patterns into the clay. (Try out the **impressions** on small scrap clay first.) You might also add small balls of clay as decoration.

– Mark an eye or add one from spare clay.
– Stamp a hole near the top of the fish so that it can be hung up when it's been fired.
2 Ask the children to make their own fish plaques.
3 Leave the fish to dry, then **biscuit-fire** them. They can be painted and varnished, or glazed and **fired** again.

Teaching points
▶ Remind the children that they must smooth down cut edges of clay or they will be very sharp when fired.
▶ Try to get them into the habit of making small experiments with impressions on pieces of scrap clay.
▶ Provide paper and pencils for those children who want to design their own fish.
▶ Stress that you expect each one to be different and decorative: tails can be curled up, fins added.
▶ Added decorations must be stuck on with **slip**.

92 Decorative owl plaques

Scope
Rolled clay work decorated with impressions

Age
8–11

Organisation
Up to half a class, depending on equipment available, working individually

Time
1–1 1/2 hours

Cross-curricular links
Science (birds)

You will need
copies of pcm 92 preferably on card; clay; wooden boards tools to make impressions with (*see* Introduction to Clay work, p.63); rolling pins; cloths; pairs of sticks; pots of slip; clay cutters (needle type); paints; glaze; varnish

pcm 92 on page 94

Purposes
● To practise rolling slabs of clay.
● To explore making patterns in clay.

Activity
1 Demonstrate making an owl plaque:
– Follow the instructions for fish plaques in idea 91, using the owl shape cut out from pcm 92 to cut round.
– Either mark the wings in the clay or add wings cut out of some of the scraps of rolled clay.
2 Ask the children to make their own owl plaques.
3 Leave the owl plaques to dry, then **biscuit-fire** them. They can then be painted and varnished, or glazed and **fired** again.

Teaching points
▶ *See* Teaching points for idea 91.

▶ Stress that each owl should be different. Allow children to individualise their work as they wish by adding claws and wings, or even a mortar board and book! You might suggest that the owls could be perched on the branch of a tree.

93 Decorative house plaques

Scope
Rolled clay work decorated with impressions

Age
8–11

Organisation
Up to half a class, depending on equipment available, working individually

Time
1–1 1/2 hours

Cross-curricular links,
Geography (the environment, houses and homes)

You will need
pieces of card up to 20 cm by 17 cm; clay; wooden boards; tools to make impressions with (*see* Introduction to Clay work, p.63); rolling pins; cloths; pairs of sticks; pots of slip; clay cutters (needle type); metal sieve; small extruding tool if available; paints; varnish; glaze; pictures of houses

Purposes
● To practise rolling slabs of clay.
● To explore making patterns in clay.

Activity
1 With the children, look at pictures of houses of all types. Talk about the different roofing and building materials.
2 Demonstrate making a house plaque:
– Follow the instructions for fish plaques in idea 91, using a house shape to cut round.
3 Ask the children to make their own house plaques. Encourage them to design their own houses and make patterns for them. (Restrict the size by providing pieces of paper no bigger than 20 cm by 17 cm.)
4 Ask the children to suggest ways to get the effect of a thatched roof, for instance, and try out some of their suggestions while they watch. Discuss with them what works well.

5 Show them how to press clay through the sieve and the extruding tool to make textured clay that might be useful for foliage, etc.
6 Leave the houses to dry, then **biscuit-fire** them. They can then be painted and varnished or **glazed** and **fired** again.

Teaching points
▶ *See* Teaching points for idea 91. Remind the children that you expect all the houses to be individual. Chimneys and other details may be added using scraps of rolled clay.
▶ Children who are experienced at clay work may like to make their houses with a ledge on the base so that they are free-standing.
▶ These houses would also make a good display for school if they were stuck on to hessian in rows of 'streets'.

94 Pressed leaf dishes

Scope
Rolled clay work decorated with impressions of real leaves

Age
5–11

Organisation
Individual work;
5–7 year-olds: groups of 6;
8–11 year-olds: up to half a class, depending on equipment available

Time
1 hour

Cross-curricular links
Science (autumn, plants)

You will need
clay; wooden boards; tools to make impressions with (*see* Introduction to Clay work, p.63); rolling pins; cloths; pairs of sticks; large leaves with interesting shapes; clay cutters (needle type); paints; varnish ; glaze

Purposes
● To practise rolling slabs of clay.
● To see the effect of making leaf **impressions** in the clay.
● To practise mixing colours to decorate the leaves.

Activity
1 Demonstrate making a pressed leaf dish:
– **Wedge** a lump of clay about as big as a woman's fist, then roll this into a ball.
– Place it on a spread-out cloth and flatten it with your hands.
– Lay the sticks, one either side of the clay, then roll it out flat with the rolling pin. (The sticks will ensure that the clay is rolled to an even thickness.)
– Place the leaf on the clay with the veins pressed into the surface and cut round it.
– Mark your initials on the reverse of the leaf, then transfer it to a wooden board.
– Smooth the cut edges of the leaf, so that they will not be sharp when they are fired.
– Curl up the edges of the leaf a little so that it forms a shallow dish; support these

curled up edges with small pieces of crumpled paper, while the clay dries.
2 Ask the children to make their own pressed leaf dishes.
3 Leave them to dry, then **biscuit-fire** them.
4 The leaves can then be painted. I would use this as an opportunity to practise mixing shades of one colour, for instance shades of orange, and get the children to dab different shades on the leaves.
5 If you decide to **glaze** the leaves, this project would make good use of 'paint on' glazes. Get the children to look at some vibrant-coloured autumn leaves first, if using shades of orange.

Teaching points
▶ Younger children will need help rolling out the clay.
▶ Remind the children that they must smooth down the cut edges of clay or they will be very sharp when **fired**.
▶ They may need help marking their initials on the back of the leaves so as not to spoil the pattern of the veins.

95 Making a coil pot

Scope
A basic technique for making pots

Age
9–11

Organisation
Groups of 6–8 working individually

Time
1–1 1/2 hours

Cross-curricular links
Geography (other lands and cultures, e.g. Africa)

You will need
clay; wooden boards; rolling pins; cloths; pairs of sticks; pots of slip; clay cutters (needle type); lolly sticks or similar modelling tools; tools to make impressions with (*see* Introduction to Clay work, p.63); circular card templates, various sizes from 10 cm to 15 cm diameter; paint brushes; paints; glaze

Purposes

- To practise rolling slabs of clay.
- To practise rolling coils of clay.
- To use these techniques to build a pot.

Activity

1 Demonstrate making a coil pot:

– **Wedge** a lump of clay about as big as a child's fist, then roll this into a ball.

– Place it on a spread-out cloth and flatten it with your hands.

– Lay the sticks one either side of the clay, then roll it out flat with the rolling pin. (The sticks will ensure that the clay is rolled to an even thickness.)

– Place a circular template on the clay and cut round the shape. This will form the base of the pot.

– Mark your initials on the reverse of the base, then transfer it to a wooden board.

– Take some small pieces of clay (about half a child's fist size) and roll them into long, even sausages or coils. (It will take a bit of practise to make even coils.)

– Put some **slip** around the edge of the rolled out base and place a coil round it on top of the slip.

– Now roll another coil and place this on top of the first one, using slip to stick the two coils together.

– Continue this until the pot is as high as you want it to be.

– Place a thin coil around the inside of the base of the pot, sticking it in with slip. This will strengthen the join at the base.

– Using a lolly stick or modelling tool, smooth down the coils inside the pot, blending them together. This will strengthen the pot considerably.

– Decorate the coils on the outside of the pot with rows of **impressed patterns**. (Try the patterns out on some scrap clay first.)

2 Ask the children to make their own coil pots.

3 Leave the pots to dry thoroughly, then **biscuit-fire** them. They can then be painted and varnished or, if they are to be used as vases, they will need glazing and **firing** again.

Teaching points

▶ Join the ends of the coils with slip. As you build the pot, avoid getting the joins in each coil directly above each other, as this will make a weakness in the pot.

▶ Coil pots can be made in any shape and size when the children become proficient at making them.

▶ The outside coils can be smoothed down too, if desired, and the pots decorated in various ways, for instance by inscribing marks in the clay.

▶ If the children are studying African pots, they may like to reproduce some of the effects found on African pottery.

▶ If you do not get the pots completed in one session, wrap them in polythene bags and store them somewhere cool for up to a week.

96 Clay dinners

Scope
Rolled clay-work plate with modelled food

Age
8–11

Organisation
Up to half class, depending on equipment available, working individually

Time
1 1/2 hours

Cross-curricular links
PSE (food, myself)

You will need
clay; wooden boards; tools to make impressions with (*see* Introduction to Clay work, p.63); rolling pins; cloths; pairs of sticks; clay cutters (needle type); plates, about 15 cm in diameter, lined with piece of thin cloth; pots of slip; paints; glaze

Purposes
● To practise rolling slabs of clay.
● To represent different textures in clay.

Activity
1 Demonstrate making a clay-work plate of food:
– **Wedge** a lump of clay about as big as a child's fist, then roll this into a ball.
– Place it on a spread-out cloth and flatten it with your hands.
– Lay the sticks one either side of the clay, then roll the clay out flat with the rolling pin.
– Place the plate on the clay and cut out around it.
– Mark your initials on the back of the clay, then transfer it to the lined plate which will support the circle in a plate shape while the clay dries.
– Smooth the edges.
– Wedge the bits of cut-off clay and use these to model some food. This can be anything from a favourite dinner to a plate of cakes.
2 Ask the children to make their own clay-work plates of food.
3 Leave the plates of food to dry, then lift them carefully off the supporting plates. Leave them for a further two or three days to ensure that they are dry underneath, then **biscuit-fire** them. They can then be painted, or painted with **glazes** and **fired** again.

Teaching points
▶ Some children will need help rolling out the clay.
▶ Remind the children that they must smooth down the cut edges of clay or their plates will be very sharp when fired.
▶ Ask the children to think carefully about the texture of the foods that they model.

Further activities
▶ The children could make clay fruit and vegetables for a harvest festival display, for instance. Provide actual fruits and vegetables for them to look at, and talk about the shapes and textures. If the children make solid round fruits, get them to hollow these out from underneath to enable the clay to dry out thoroughly, or they could make them in self-hardening clay and just paint them to finish them off, matching the colours as carefully as they can to the real fruits.

97 Clay figures

Scope
Activity for 9–11 year-olds who are experienced in clay work

Age
9–11

Organisation
Up to half a class, depending on space and equipment, working individually

Time
Making figures: 1 1/2 hours; painting and glazing: 1 hour

Cross-curricular links
PSE (myself)

You will need
clay; wooden boards tools to make impressions (*see* Introduction to Clay work, p.63); pots of slip; old table knives; metal sieve; rolling pins; cloths; paints; glazes

Purpose
● To make human figures, practising several important clay techniques.

Activity
1 Demonstrate making a clay figure:
– **Wedge** a lump of clay about as big as a child's fist, then roll this into a ball, then into a sausage.
– Gently shape this into a torso with a head and neck formed at one end.
– Take another lump of clay, about as big as the first one, and wedge this before rolling it into another sausage shape.
– Cut this in two and shape the two pieces into similarly shaped legs.
– Join these to the base of the torso, using **slip**. (Do this with the figure lying down.) Now take a smaller piece of clay and form the arms from this in the same way as the legs.
– Decide what position the figure is to be in (*see* Teaching points). Gently move the figure into the required position.
– Add clothes (use small pieces of modelled or thinly rolled clay stuck on with slip), and model the features and hair. Add any other details, such as a book to read, etc.
2 Ask the children to make their own clay figures.
3 Leave the figures until they are thoroughly dry, then **biscuit-fire** them. Paint or **glaze** as desired.

Teaching points

► Remind the children to try out textured effects for hair, etc., on a piece of spare clay.

► Stress that arms and leg joints must be made with great care or the limbs will fall off, and get the children to check this.

► Standing figures are extremely difficult to make unless they are supported by, for instance, a small clay cupboard. Suggest to the children that the figures are either lying or sitting. Seated figures could have their legs dangling over the edge of the board or table, but you will need somewhere suitable to dry out this type of figure.

► Get the children to pose for one another if necessary so that they can observe how the body bends.

► Sunbathers make a good theme for lying figures.

Further activities

► Children could draw people in different positions as a basis for modelling clay figures. Get the children to pose for one another for quick sketches, asking them to concentrate on the proportions of the body and the position of the limbs.

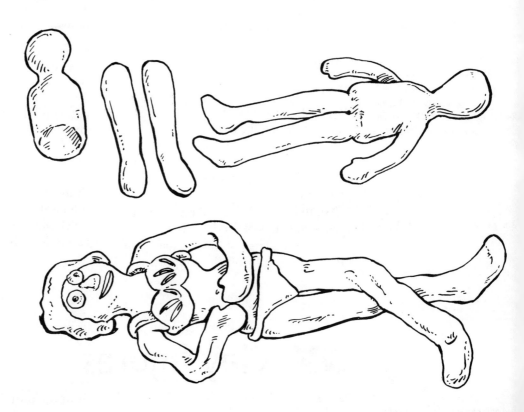

Weaving

See pcm on page 82 for examples of weaving

Weaving at primary level offers the children a chance to begin exploring a subject that is an art form, a craft and an industrial process. In a weaving activity, children will begin to learn about the process of weaving, develop fine motor skills and sort and handle a wide range of coloured and textured materials.

The activities in this section (ideas 98–100) rely for interest on the provision of a variety of wools and other materials. An appeal to parents should provide a 'harvest' of knitting wools which would make a good start. Often interesting odd balls of knitting wool can be acquired from charity shops, too. See below for suggestions for other materials to add to the collection.

If you don't have room for each child to make and use a loom, having one or two 'class weavings' on the go over a period of weeks is one way of offering the children the opportunity to experience this activity. Children could be invited to add to the weaving when they have a few minutes to spare. You might even choose a theme to complement a class project: for example, if you are teaching the tropical rainforest, you might initiate a weaving which concentrates on the feeling of the dark jungle with patches of brilliant colour. If you are doing 'the seaside' with younger children, you might represent the textures of sea and sand.

Above all, encourage the children to enjoy using the variety of materials you've collected.

Basic equipment

Depending on activity select from:
- wool of all types, textures and colours, including strong nylon wool, strips of cut and torn fabric, raffia, string, rope, polythene carrier bags cut into strips, crepe paper, lace, ribbon, tinsel, twigs, feathers, dried grasses, tissue paper twisted into ropes, etc.
- strong cardboard boxes
- garden canes or dried prunings from shrubs
- tapestry needles for threading up looms

98 Woven wall-hangings

Scope
Weaving on a homemade box loom with a variety of materials

Age
5–11

Organisation
5–7 year-olds: class weaving (*see* Teaching points); 8–11 year-olds: individual work in whole class

Time
Making loom: 1 hour; weaving: 2 hours (2 sessions)

You will need
copies of pcm 98; cardboard boxes; strong nylon wool; wide selection of weaving materials with variety of textures, such as: strips of fabric cut and torn, wool of all types, raffia, string, polythene carrier bags cut into strips, crepe paper, lace, ribbon, tinsel, twigs, etc.

pcm 98 on page 95

Purposes
● To offer the children the experience of weaving.
● To offer the children the opportunity to handle a variety of textured materials.

Activity
Session 1
1 With the children, look at different fabrics. Talk about the warp and weft threads that make up the basis of a piece of woven fabric. Look at the range of materials you have accumulated and talk briefly about the different qualities they possess.
2 Demonstrate how to make a box loom, following the instructions on pcm 98.
3 Thread up the loom with strong nylon wool that can be pulled fairly taut.
4 Ask 8–11 year-olds to make and thread up their own looms, either at school or at home.

Session 2
5 Demonstrate weaving:
– Show the basic principle of going 'under and over' the warp threads on one row, 'over and under' on the next. (Shuttles are not needed for weaving on this scale and with these materials.)
– Allow the ends of the material to hang out at the sides of the weaving. This will add to the decorative effect of these hangings. The ends can be tied in pairs to make the hangings more secure.

6 Ask the children to make their own woven wall-hangings.
7 When the wall-hangings are finished, use a craft knife to cut the weaving off the boxes, leaving a thin band of cardboard at the top and bottom. This will enable the weaving to be hung up easily. You will probably need to do this for the children. Some children may prefer to leave their weaving on the box-loom for display.

Teaching points
▶ Most children grasp the idea of weaving, but some need extra attention to avoid getting in a muddle.
▶ Talk to the children as they work about contrasts in the different materials they are using.
▶ You may like to suggest that they choose a theme for their weaving. Some suggestions are: the seasons, a rainbow, yellow (or other colour) weaving, a cornfield in summer, a snowy day. Emphasise that you are not expecting a pictoral interpretation of the theme, just the colours and feelings suggested by them.
▶ You could make a large box loom for younger children and have this in the classroom as an ongoing project. All the children could have a go.
▶ Weaving with natural materials that they have helped collect; plants, twigs, etc., would also be good with young children.

99 Circular woven mats

Scope
Weaving on circular cardboard looms with a variety of materials

Age
5–11

Organisation
5–7 year-olds: 8 children working with adult supervision; 8–11 year-olds: up to half a class working, individually

Time
Making loom: 1/2 hour; weaving time: 1 hour (2 sessions)

Purposes
● To offer the children the experience of weaving.
● To offer the children the opportunity to handle a variety of different textured materials.

Activity
Session 1
1 With the children, look at the range of materials you have accumulated and talk about the different qualities they possess.
2 Demonstrate how to make a circular loom, following the instructions on pcm 99.

3 Demonstrate threading up the loom:
– Choose any strong nylon wool that can be pulled fairly taut and make a small sl for the wool in the inner circle of the loom.
– Pull the end of the wool through the slit to hold it in place while you wind th wool round the loom about 19 times. Y need to finish with an odd number of threads. (The number of threads can vary according to the size of the loom.)
– Tie the ends of the threads together.

You will need
copies of pcm 99;
strong cardboard boxes;
strong nylon wool;
selection of weaving materials with a
wide variety of textures and colours,
such as: strips of fabric, cut and torn,
wool of all types, raffia, string,
polythene carrier bags of all colours cut
into strips, crepe paper, lace, ribbon,
tinsel, twigs, etc.

pcm 99 on page 96

4 Ask the children to make and thread up their looms, either in school or at home. (*See* Teaching points for 5–7 year-olds.)
Session 2
5 Demonstrate weaving on the circular loom:
– Starting in the centre of the loom, demonstrate going 'under and over' the warp threads on the loom then 'over and under', working round and round it.
– When you run out of thread or wool, tie another piece on the end.
– Tuck the knotted ends under the weaving as it progresses.
– It's best to choose a fairly fine thread or material for the inner section of the work and chunkier materials for the outer edge.
6 The children do their own weaving on their circular looms.

Teaching points
▶ Most children grasp the idea of weaving, but some need extra attention to avoid getting in a muddle.
▶ Talk to the children as they work about contrasts in the different materials they are using.
▶ You may like to suggest that they choose a theme for their weaving. (*See* idea 98 for some suggestions but as this is a circular weaving, you may also like to suggest some ideas linked to a circular theme, such as 'Sunflowers'.)
▶ Looms need to be made of stiff, strong card, difficult for children to cut, such as cardboard cut from boxes. Because of this pcm 99 is designed as an instruction sheet that might be sent home so that parents could help cut out the looms. 5–7 year-olds will need to have their looms made in advance by the teacher or a helper.

100 Stick weaving

Scope
Colourful weavings done on a pair of sticks

Age
9–11

Organisation
Up to half a class, working individually

Time
1 1/2 hours

Cross-curricular links
Geography (crafts of other lands)

You will need
fairly straight sticks about 30 cm long for each child (garden canes or dried prunings from garden shrubs); varied selection of knitting wools; craft books showing traditional South American stick weaving

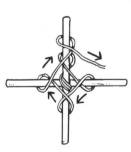

Purpose
● To make an interesting woven artifact, using a variety of threads.

Activity
1 With the children, look at pictures of *ojos de dios* or *eyes of god* if you can find some illustrations in a craft book. Talk about how they are traditional in South America from Mexico to Peru as good luck symbols. They are often put over the cribs of newborn babies to wish them good luck and good health.
2 Demonstrate the **stick weaving**:
– Hold the sticks together, then bind them together securely in the centre.
– Open them out to form a cross and bind the yarn round the centre of the cross shape to hold it in position.
– Tie a length of your chosen yarn on to the loose end of the binding yarn and start to work round the frame, winding the yarn over each stick in turn.
– Turn the frame a quarter turn each time you bind a stick. Continue round and round the four sticks that form the frame, and soon you will see a pattern start to appear.
– Change the colour of the yarn when you want to, by tying a new colour to the end of the previous thread.

3 Ask the children to do their own stick weaving.

Teaching points
▶ Talk to the children about contrasts of colour and texture as the weavings progress. They might like to work to a colour scheme, if the selection of yarns allows this.
▶ It is best to start with finer yarns in the centre of the weaving, and use thicker ones on the outside. Tell the children to stop with least 3 cm of stick still showing. Tie the end on to a stick.
▶ The ends of the sticks could be decorated with small tassels. To make these, wind some yarn around a piece of stiff card about six or seven cm long. Slide the bundle off the card and bind it tightly at one end. Snip the loops at the other end. Bind it to the end of a stick.
▶ The weavings could be decorated with buttons, sequins and small pieces of felt.
▶ Make loops on the top stick with which to hang up the weavings.
▶ Small fine versions of this weaving could be made using wooden kebab skewers with the points cut off for the sticks. You would need to bind these with fairly fine wool. These small versions would make attractive Christmas tree decorations.

Printing

18   Engraved
      leaf print border

9   Owl print using junk and feather-
     shaped potato block

10   Vase of leaves
      and berries using
      leaf-shaped potato
      block

21   Collagraph print

24   Drawn mono-print

100 ideas for Art ©HarperCollins*Publishers* 19

Collage work

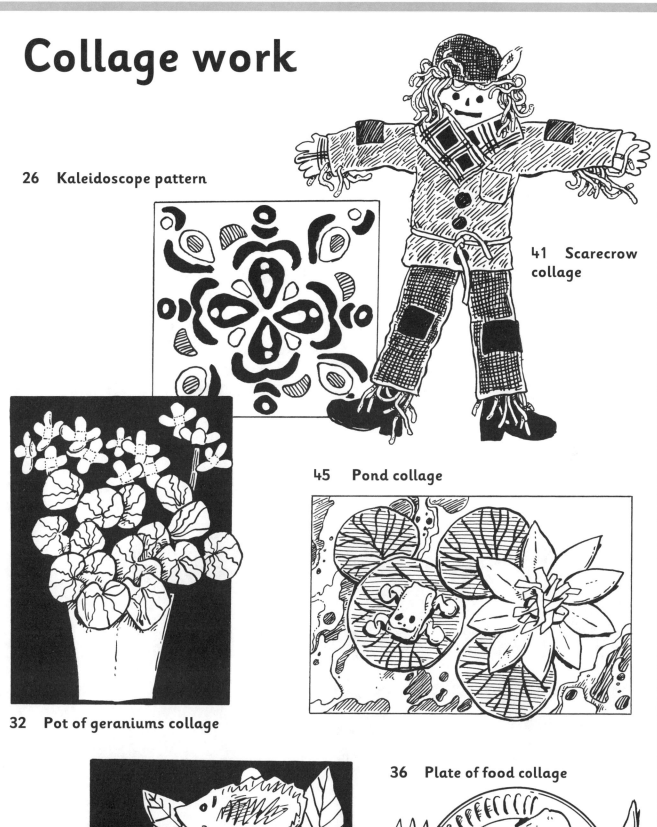

26   Kaleidoscope pattern

41   Scarecrow collage

32   Pot of geraniums collage

45   Pond collage

33   Autumn leaf collage

36   Plate of food collage

Painting

Brush techniques

58 Pastel word picture

57 Pastel techniques

Drawing

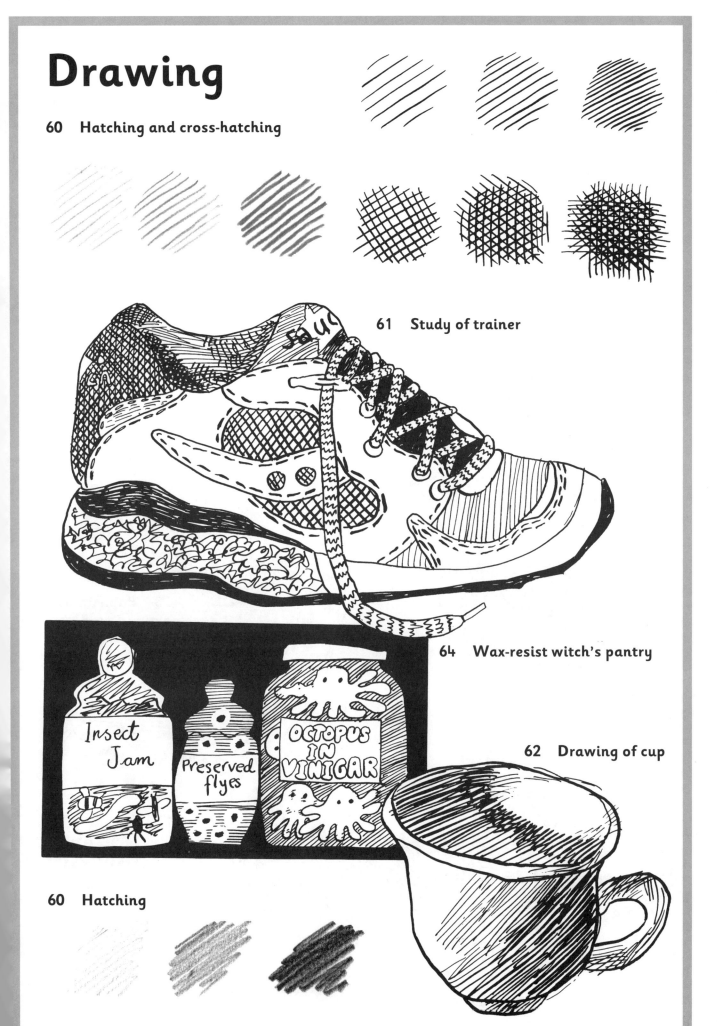

60 Hatching and cross-hatching

61 Study of trainer

64 Wax-resist witch's pantry

Insect Jam

Preserved flyes

OCTOPUS IN VINIGAR

62 Drawing of cup

60 Hatching

Model-making and papier-mâché work

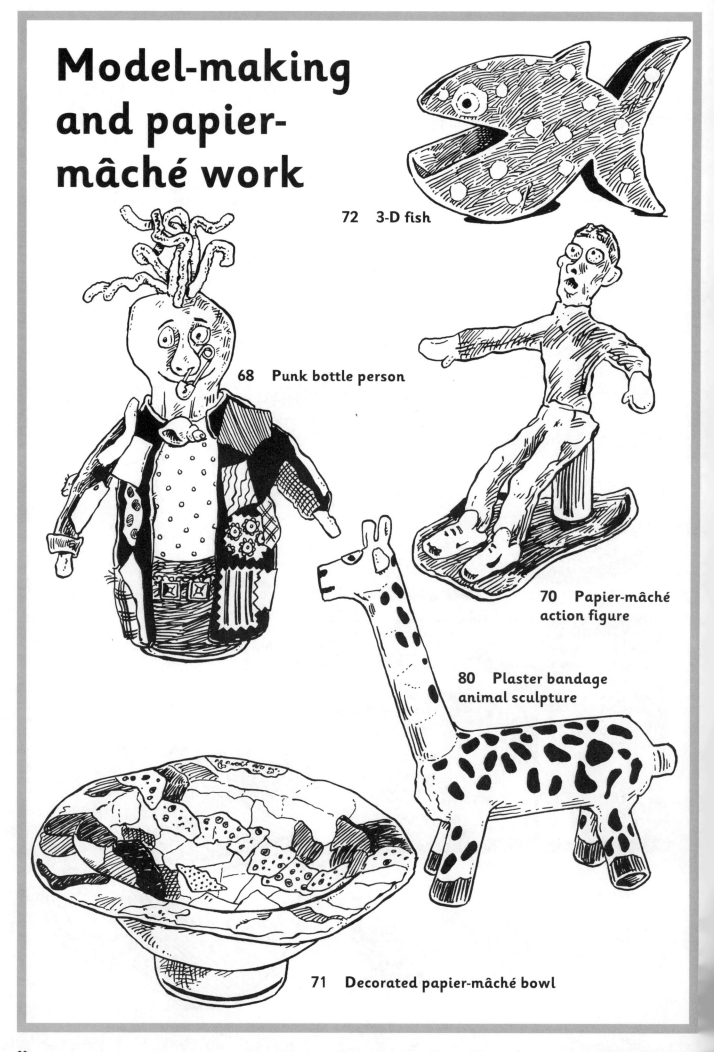

72   3-D fish

68   Punk bottle person

70   Papier-mâché action figure

80   Plaster bandage animal sculpture

71   Decorated papier-mâché bowl

Clay work

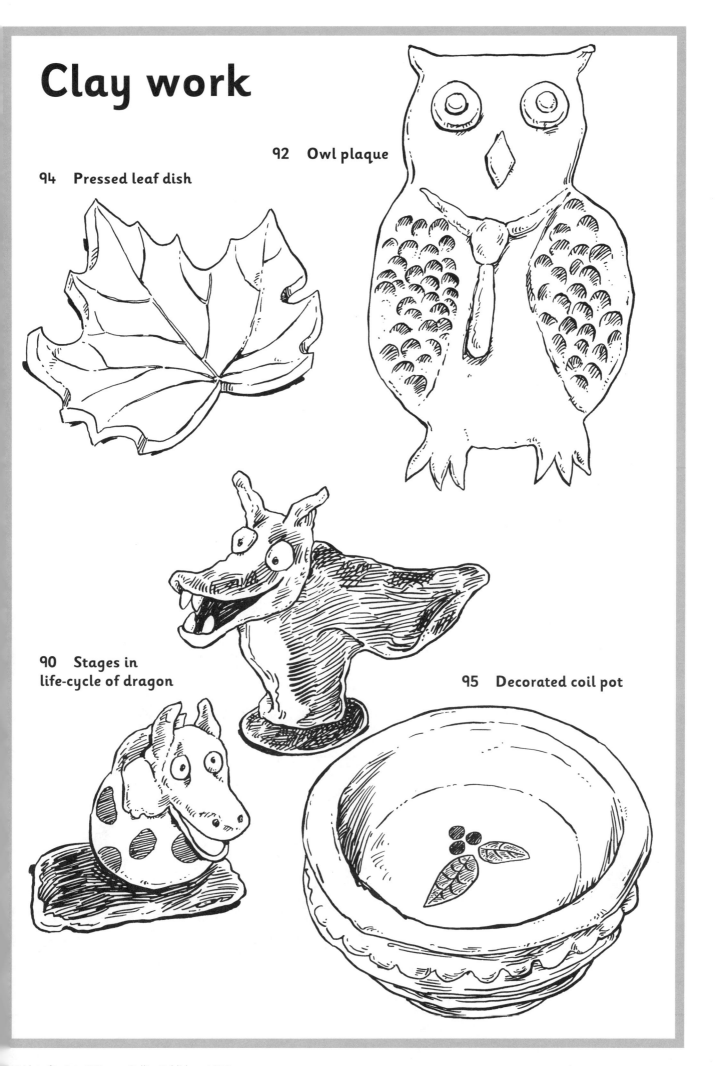

94   Pressed leaf dish

92   Owl plaque

90   Stages in
life-cycle of dragon

95   Decorated coil pot

Weaving

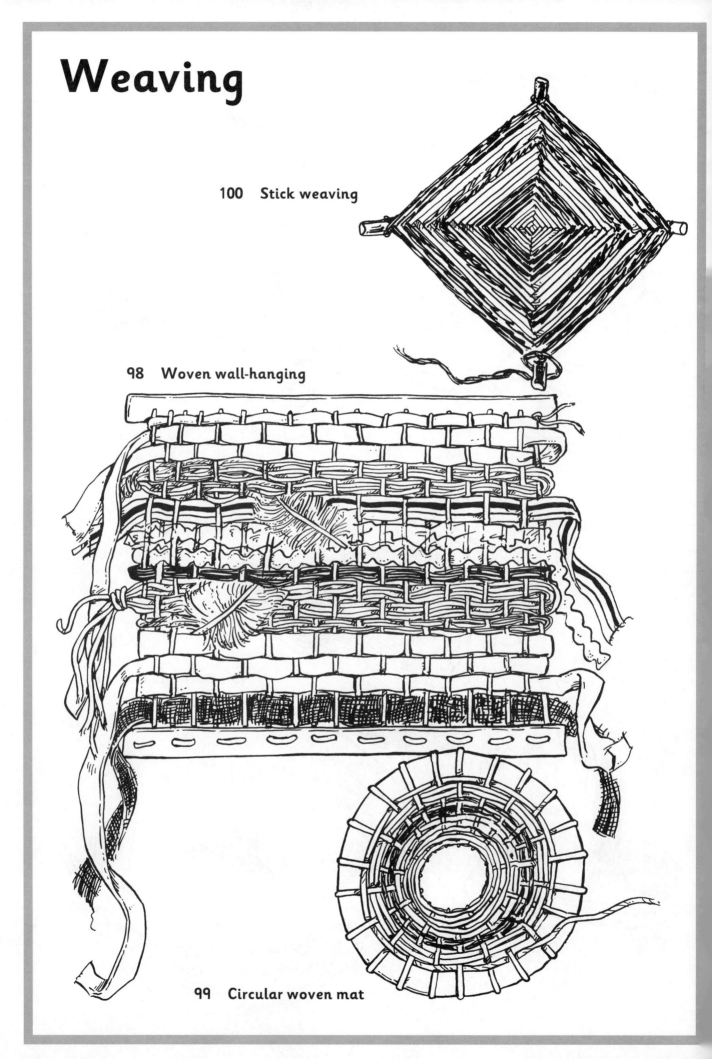

100 **Stick weaving**

98 **Woven wall-hanging**

99 **Circular woven mat**

Printed lizards on leaves

Can be enlarged when copying.

Flower patterns

sunflower centre

▶ Cut 1 out of stiff paper or card.

sunflower petal

▶ Cut 8 for each flower.

▶ Stick the petals round the centres.

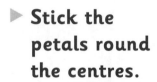

dahlia centre

▶ Cut 1 out of stiff paper.

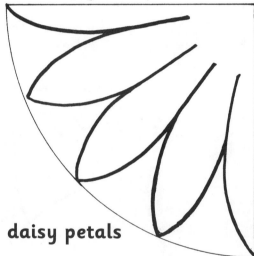

daisy petals

▶ Lay on a circle of paper folded into four. Cut out.

dahlia petal

▶ Cut lots out of folded tissue paper.

camellia petal

▶ Cut 6 or 8 for each flower.

camellia centre

▶ Cut 1 out of stiff paper.

100 ideas for Art ©HarperCollins*Publishers* 1998

Patterns for waterlilies and dragonfly

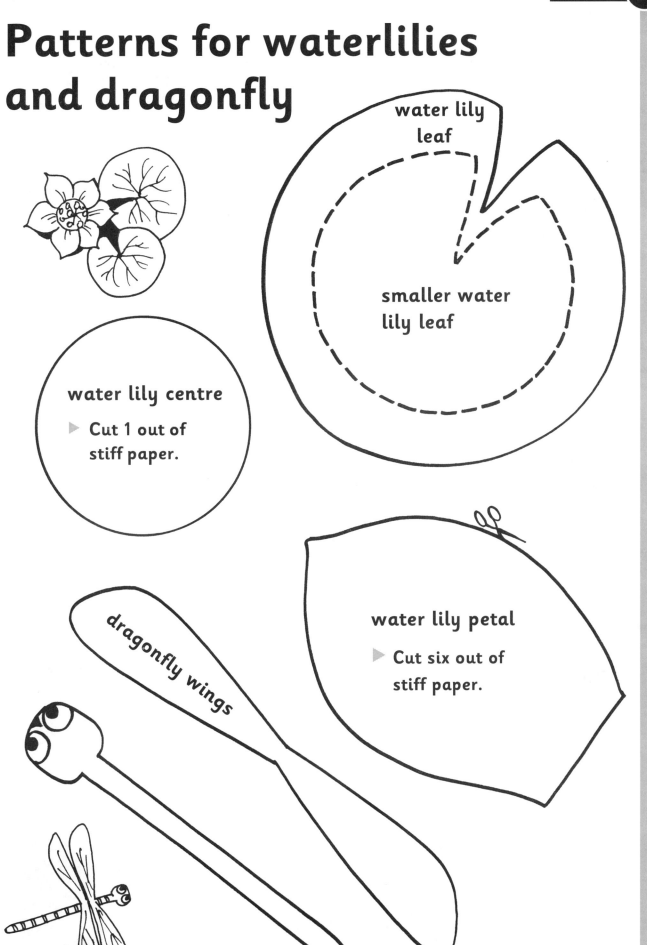

water lily leaf

smaller water lily leaf

water lily centre

▶ **Cut 1 out of stiff paper.**

water lily petal

▶ **Cut six out of stiff paper.**

dragonfly wings

dragonfly body

Silhouette collages

The witches' spell

Fillet of a fenny snake

In the cauldron boil and bake;

Eye of newt, and toe of frog,

Wool of bat, and tongue of dog,

Adder's fork and blind-worm's sting,

Lizard's leg and howlet's wing –

For a chain of powerful trouble,

Like a hell-broth boil and bubble.

Double, double toil and trouble;

Fire burn, and cauldron bubble.

William Shakespeare
Macbeth, Act IV scene 1

howlet – owl

The old boots

Hatching and cross-hatching excercises

▲ Try to match the patch of hatching.

▲ Use a 2B pencil.

▲ Draw lots of fine lines close together.

press very lightly ——→ press more heavily ——→ press heavily

▲ Now try some cross-hatching. This is also useful for showing areas of shade.

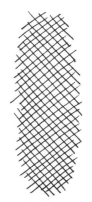

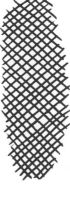

Drawing a portrait

▶ **Draw the other half of this portrait.**

▶ **Draw the other half of this portrait.**

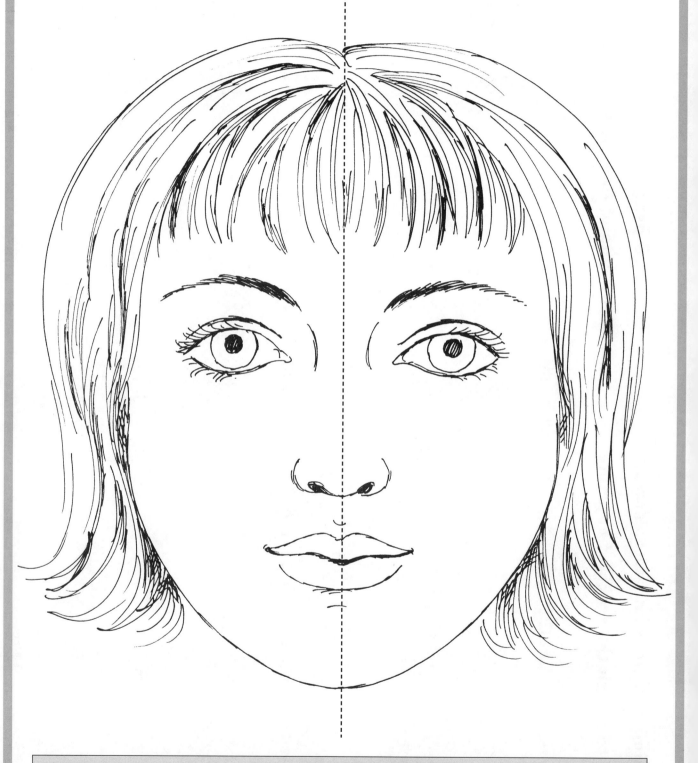

Mask half the portrait with a piece of paper before photocopying.
Give the left-hand half portrait to right-handed children and vice versa.

100 ideas for Art ©HarperCollins*Publishers* 1998

Drawing a simple still life

▶ Practise drawing some ellipses in pencil at the side.

▶ Then complete the pots and jar.

▶ Practise drawing some ellipses in pencil at the side.

▶ Then complete the pots and jar.

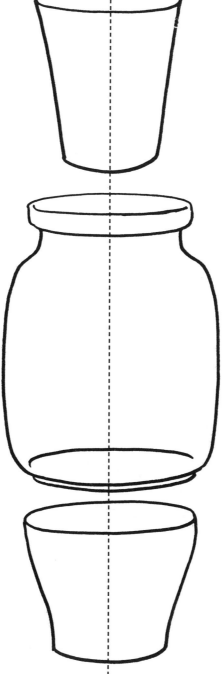
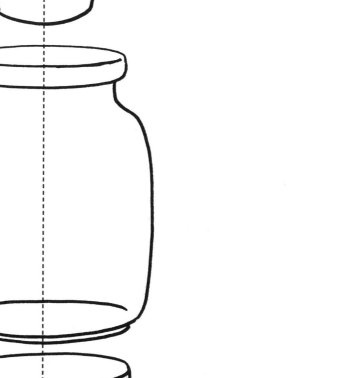

Mask half the pots and jar with a piece of paper before photocopying. Give the left-hand half picture to right-handed children and vice versa.

3-D fish

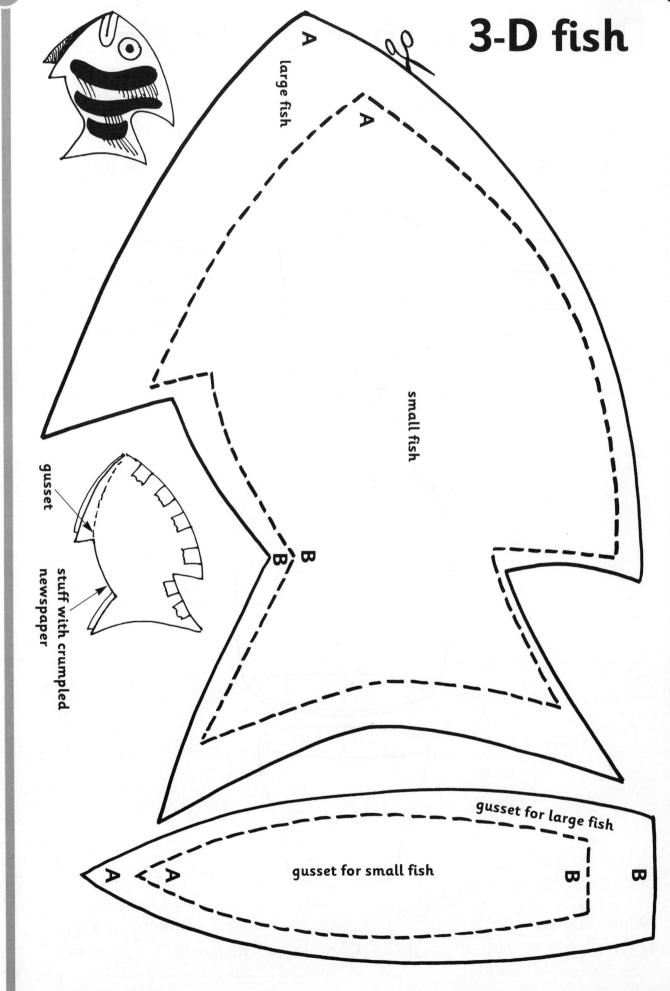

large fish

A

A

small fish

gusset

stuff with crumpled newspaper

B

B

gusset for large fish

gusset for small fish

A

A

B

B

100 ideas for Art ©HarperCollins*Publishers* 1998

Model houses

Roof

▶ Cut 1.
Fold along the
dotted line.

Front and end of house

Back and end of house

▶ Cut 2 and fold along
the dotted lines.

glue along here

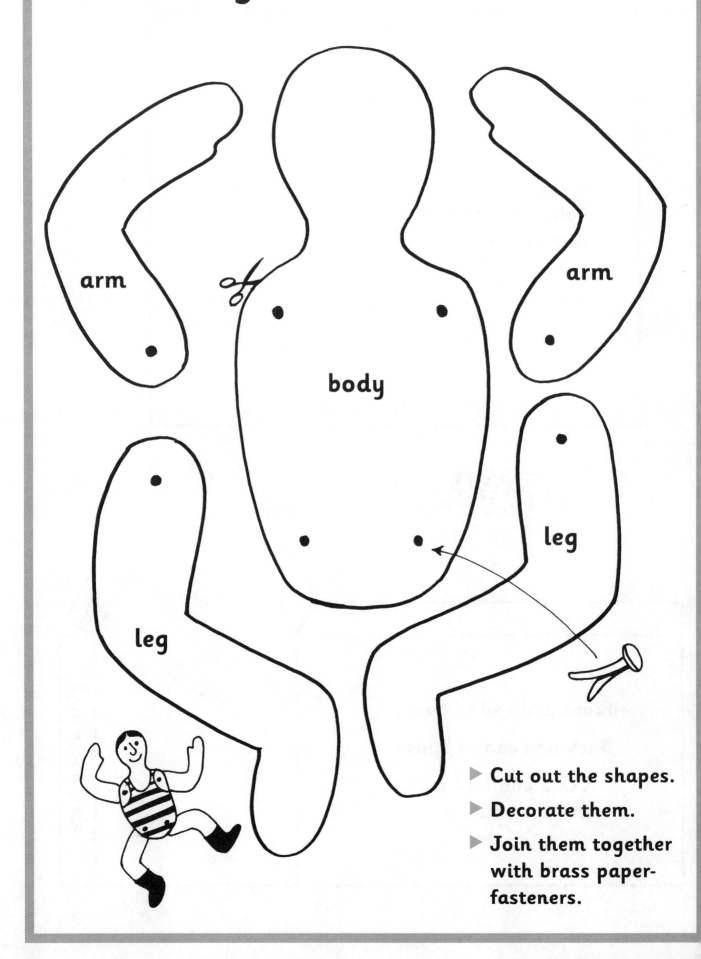

Model figures

arm

arm

body

leg

leg

▶ Cut out the shapes.

▶ Decorate them.

▶ Join them together with brass paper-fasteners.

100 ideas for Art ©HarperCollins*Publishers* 199

Christmas angels

▷ **Cut out the shapes.**

▷ **Make the head like this.**

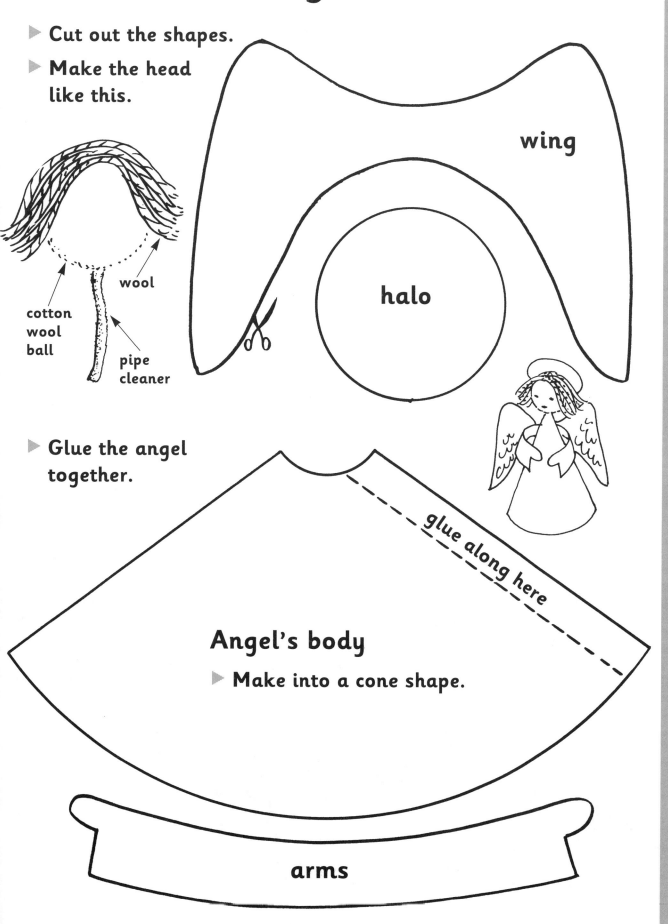

wool

cotton wool ball

pipe cleaner

wing

halo

▷ **Glue the angel together.**

glue along here

Angel's body

▷ **Make into a cone shape.**

arms

Owl and fish plaques

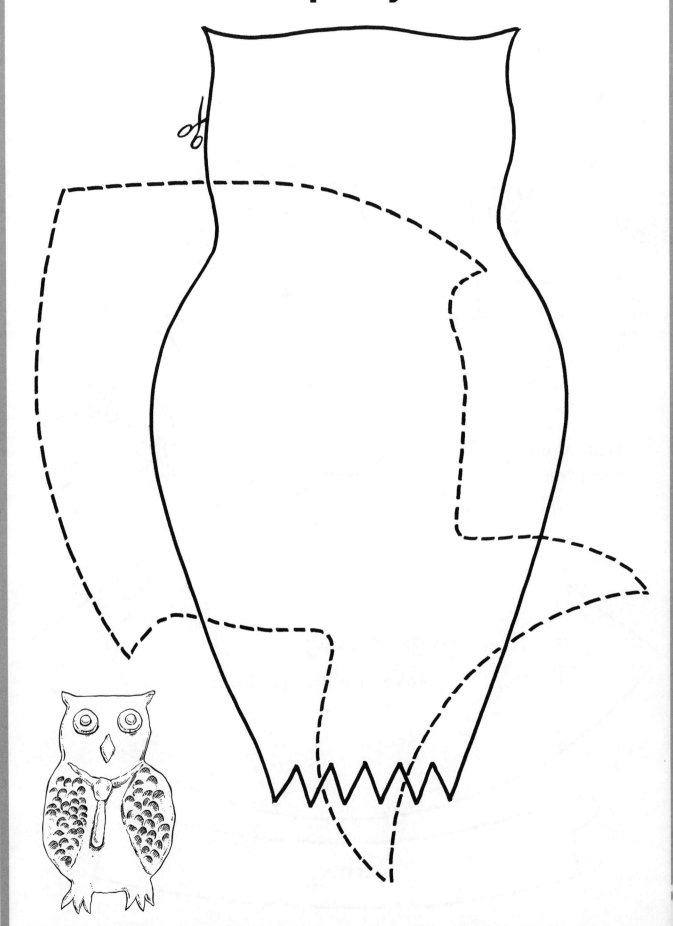

Woven wall-hangings

Making a box loom

You will need

• large flattish box with lip, if possible

• bradawl or very big needle to make holes

• strong nylon wool and large needle

▶ Mark dots 1.5 cm apart and 2 cm from the edge of the box.

tie wool at beginning

go under here between holes when threading up

▶ Make holes where you've marked the dots with a bradawl or a very big needle. Get help if you need it!

▶ Using strong nylon wool and a big needle, thread from one end to the other. Join the wool as necessary. (The joins won't show when you've finished.)

Circular woven mats

Making a circular loom

You will need

- stiff cardboard
- scissors
- strong nylon wool

▶ Cut the loom out of stiff cardboard.

▶ Cut a hole in the centre.

▶ Wind wool round the loom an odd number of times: about 19 times.

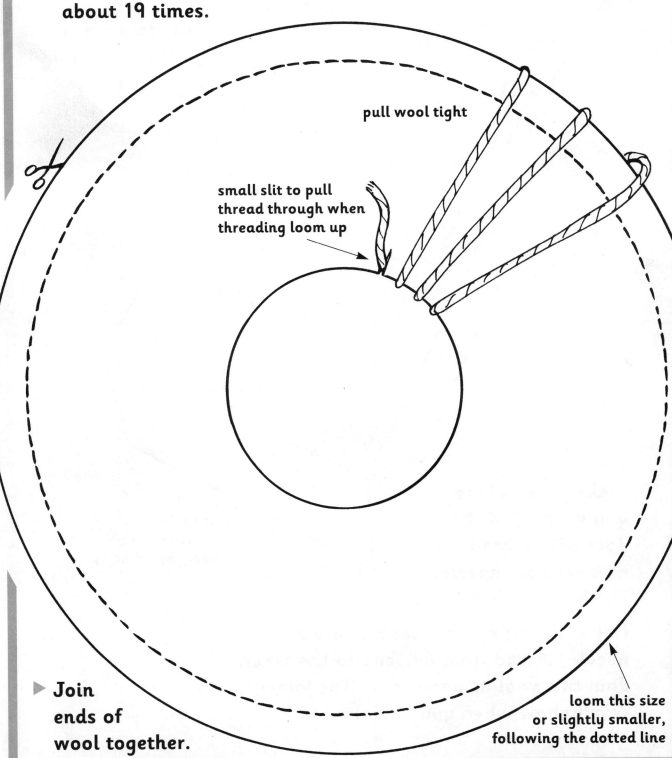

pull wool tight

small slit to pull thread through when threading loom up

▶ Join ends of wool together.

loom this size or slightly smaller, following the dotted line

100 ideas for Art ©HarperCollins*Publishers* 19